Seven
Discoveries

For You, the Seeker

Kai Mark

SEVEN DISCOVERIES
For You, the Seeker

Graphics by Scott Lee.

ISBN-10: 1897373-93-7
ISBN-13: 9781897373-93-4

Printed by Word Alive Press
131 Cordite Road, Winnipeg, MB R3W 1S1
www.wordalivepress.ca

WORD ALIVE PRESS
Just Write!

Printed in Canada.

INTRODUCTION

Ever since I was born, my parents brought me to church. In fact, my parents were so religious that I remember attending three different churches every Sunday for several years of my life. As I grew older, I was becoming tired of the institutionalized church. I found the programs in the church boring with little relevance to my life. I made up my mind at a young age that I was going to attend church much less when I grew older. However, that indifferent attitude I had about church changed when I met the Lord. I came to understand that an authentic, interactive, satisfying relationship with God is very different from the stuffy religion I grew up with.

Religion in general is often complex. Every belief system has many rules and regulations. Even if you claim to believe in nothing, there are still laws dictating what is right and what is wrong. The institutionalized church has made faith so impersonal and political that many people want no part of it. Christianity was never meant to be so difficult. Believing in God was never intended to be so complicated. Ever since I was a young teen, I thought of how having a relationship with God could be presented in a simple, precise, and logical manner. *Seven Discoveries* was a result of many years of reflection on this matter.

This book is an overview of seven important building blocks to the foundation of Christianity. Courses have been given in colleges and universities regarding the topics in each chapter, yet I tried to address each topic with a balance of diligence and simplicity that even a young teen can understand. The purpose of this book is to introduce Jesus to the seeker in an uncomplicated, but informative manner. Anyone who would like to engage deeper into a topic is encouraged to freely do their research.

We are all on a spiritual journey. Some do not realize that they are on a journey. Others deny ever being interested in their journey. Some feel that they are seeking in their journey, while others feel they have traveled far. I certainly am not even close to arriving at the end of my spiritual journey. I still have much to discover, digest, and do in my relationship with God. God is a reality in my life and it is my desire that you will discover Him. Wherever you are in your spiritual path, I pray that *Seven Discoveries* will help you on your journey. May you discover the Lord and be blessed in your journey!

Kai Mark

TABLE OF CONTENTS

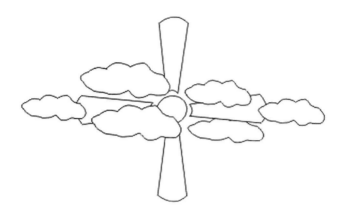

CHAPTER ONE
Discover God

Who is God? Is it reasonable to believe that God exists? How can anyone know for sure that God exists? Can we logically conclude that God exists without a leap of faith? Is there evidence that supports His existence? Is God relevant to my life?

People today are seeking out a purpose for life. Many who have tried to find it in achievements, money, popularity, relationships, fame, and other avenues find themselves on a dead end street. There is emptiness in life when God is not a factor.

A story was once told of a police officer who saw a man standing on a bridge contemplating suicide. As the policeman approached the suicidal man, the officer asked to be given ten minutes of his time to convince him that life was worth living. After ten minutes, the man could then try to convince the officer why he thought life was not worth living. If, at the end of twenty minutes, the policeman could not persuade the man, he would let him jump. It was said that after twenty minutes of discussion together on the purpose of life, the officer and the man joined hands and both jumped off the bridge.

God is a significant factor in our meaning and purpose in life. In fact, when we move closer towards God in our spiritual journey, we will discover that is all about God. Our purpose in life was never about us.

But then, how can we know that God exists? Philosophers and theologians—from Plato, Aristotle, Augustine, and Aquinas to Descartes, Kant, Kierkegaard, and Schaeffer, among others—have been in deep discussions concerning the existence of God for centuries. We can glean from some of their thoughts and mental reasonings that God exists. The following are philosophical discussions that provide evidence for the existence of God. The purpose of highlighting this evidence is not to engage in deep philosophical discussions about the existence of God, but to assure the reader that believing in God is not an anti-intellectual pursuit.

The Evidences for the Existence of God

The Evidence from Cause and Effect

Plato observed that all things in this universe move.[1] Whatever moves is either moved by something else, or is self-moved. There are self-movers and a Supreme self-mover known as God. Aristotle, building on Plato's reasoning of a Supreme self-mover, argued that this pointed to a First Cause.[2] For every effect, there is a cause. There is an Ultimate Cause, or a First Cause, which many call God.

Assuming that we live in this enormous moving universe, as Plato and Aristotle reasoned, then there must be a Mover that moves the universe—a Supreme self-mover or an Ultimate Cause we call "God." The psalmist wrote, *"The heavens declare the glory of God; the skies proclaim the work of his hands. Day after day they pour forth speech; night after night they display knowledge"* (Psalms 19:1-2). When one sees the vastness of the universe, one must begin to ponder whether it existed by chance or by the cause of a Supreme Creator.

---

[1] Plato, *The Collected Dialogues.*
[2] Aristotle, *Metaphysics,* Book XII, ch. 8.

The Evidence from Design

William Paley (1743-1805), the philosopher, made the observation that a watch with all its complex design must have a watchmaker.[3] Following the same thought, one must conclude from seeing the numerous delightful designs in the universe that there must be a Master Designer. Where there is a picture, there is an artist; where there is a design, there is a designer.

When you look under a microscope, you can distinguish the differences between a plant cell and an animal cell by their design. Our universe is full of beauty, order, and symmetry. It actually takes more faith to believe that this universe came about by chance than to believe in a Master Designer. The psalmist said, *"In the beginning you laid the foundations of the earth, and the heavens are the work of your hands"* (Psalm 102:25).

The Evidence from Morality

Everyday we make moral judgments. Everyday we decide what is right or wrong. Each one of us has some standard of right and wrong that makes us a moral being. The fact that moral laws are part of the human tapestry of society gives evidence that we are created beings of a divine plan rather than creatures of random chance. The philosopher Immanuel Kant (1724-1804) wrote, "Two things fill the mind with ever new and increasing admiration and awe ... the starry heavens above me and the moral law within me."[4]

The moral law within the hearts of men lends evidence to the existence of God. The Apostle Paul wrote, *"Since they show that the requirements of the law are written on their hearts, their consciences also bearing witness, and their thoughts now accusing, now even defending them"* (Romans 2:15).

---

[3] William Paley, *The Works of William Paley*, (London: William Smith, 1842) 25 ff
[4] Immanuel Kant, *Critique of Practical Reason,* 166.

The Evidence from the Bible

The Bible begins with God. *"In the beginning God created the heavens and the earth"* (Genesis 1:1). The Bible does not start by trying to explain or prove God's existence. It just assumes the existence of God.

The Bible also claims to be the Word of God. *"For the word of God is living and active. Sharper than any double-edged sword, it penetrates even to dividing soul and spirit, joints and marrow; it judges the thoughts and attitudes of the heart"* (Hebrews 4:12). If the Bible is truly the Word of God, then it is tremendous evidence for the existence of God. The real issue is whether the Bible is the inspired Word of God or not. This will be the topic for our next chapter.

The Evidence from Jesus

Jesus, the most respected of all spiritual leaders, spoke of and related to God as His Father. He said, *"For God so loved the world that he gave his one and only Son, that whoever believes in him shall not perish but have eternal life"* (John 3:16). Jesus claimed that He and the Father are so close that when one gets to know Jesus, he or she knows the Father as well. Jesus told His disciples that the way to know God the Father is through Himself. Jesus said, *"I am the way and the truth and the life. No one comes to the Father except through me. If you really knew me, you would know my Father as well. From now on, you do know him and have seen him"* (John 14:6-7).

There are other evidences that could be brought up for discussion to support the existence of God. However, the purpose of this section is to show that it is not unintelligent to believe in God. Seekers are encouraged to search and find more evidence of God for themselves.

The Attributes of God

When Christians say that they believe in God, what kind of God are they talking about? God brings up all kinds of images in all kinds of cultures. Some people see God as an angry tyrant to be avoided. Others see God as a cosmic Santa Claus, checking his list to see who's naughty or nice. There are those who believe God created the world and went on vacation. There are others who are afraid to live, because they think God is there to pounce on their every mistake. What kind of God are Christians talking about? What are the characteristics of man that are attributed to God? The following are some key snapshot pictures of the God of the Bible.

God is One

The God of the Bible, the God of Abraham, Isaac, and Jacob, is one God. He is not God among gods. There are no other true gods. *"This is what the LORD says—Israel's King and Redeemer, the LORD Almighty: I am the first and I am the last; apart from me there is no God"* (Isaiah 44:6). *"The LORD our God, the LORD is one"* (Deuteronomy 6:4).

God is Triune God

The Bible clearly teaches that there is only one God. However, the Godhead is described as three persons: the Father, the Son, and the Holy Spirit. There is overwhelming evidence in Scripture that shows us that God is the Father, God is the Son, and God is the Holy Spirit—yet one God. This is a mystery about God that would take an eternity for us to truly comprehend.

A logical question to start with is: "Did God create man or did man create God?" If man created God, then he would create a Supreme Being that is within his own understanding. The evidence of man creating god is seen in idolatry. Men who create god or gods create beings they can picture. However, if God created man and revealed Himself, then the finite mind of man begins comprehending the infinite nature of God.

$$\begin{array}{ccc} & \textbf{Father} & \\ & \| & \\ \times & \textbf{God} & \times \\ \textbf{Son} & \neq & \textbf{Holy Spirit} \end{array}$$

5

We see in Scripture that God is the Father. Jesus taught us to pray to *"our Father in heaven"* (Matthew 6:9). We also see in Scripture that God is the Son. Jesus claimed to be God when He said, *"I and the Father are one"* (John 10:30). The Jews at the time knew what Jesus was saying. They tried to stone Jesus *"for blasphemy, because you [Jesus], a mere man, claim to be God"* (John 10:33). And thirdly, Scripture reveals to us that the Holy Spirit is God. *"Now the Lord is the Spirit, and where the Spirit of the Lord is, there is freedom"* (2 Corinthians 3:17).

God is Eternal

God is free to act within the limitations of time and beyond the limitations of time. He is the Author of time and exists beyond time. *"Before the mountains were born or you brought forth the earth and the world, from everlasting to everlasting you are God"* (Psalm 90:2).

God is Infinite

Another attribute of God is that He is infinite. He transcends all limitations that time and space imposes. God has always existed without restrictions. He reveals Himself as *"I am who I am"* (Exodus 3:14).

God is Everywhere Present

God is described as *omnipresent*—meaning *everywhere present*. This is another description of how the infinite God relates to finite space and time. The psalmist understood this when he wrote, *"Where can I go from your Spirit? Where can I flee from your presence? If I go up to the heavens, you are there; if I make my bed in the depths, you are there"* (Psalms 139:7-8).

God is All-Powerful

God is described as *omnipotent*—meaning *all-powerful*. The infinite power of God is seen in the existence of all things as a result of His will. The will of God is unlimited in contrast to the restrictions of the will of man. *"Great is our Lord and mighty in power; his under-standing has no limit"* (Psalm 147:5).

God is All-Knowing

God is described as *omniscient*—meaning *all-knowing*. In contrast to the finite mind of man, the omniscience of God comprehends all things, whether they are things in the past, present, or future. He also understands the things that are possible, as well as the actual things. The Lord said, *"I make known the end from the beginning, from anc-ient times, what is still to come"* (Isaiah 46:10).

God is Unchanging

God in His being is not capable of change in His quality of being. He could not be less or more than He already is. He said, *"I the LORD do not change"* (Malachi 3:6). God is described as *"the Father of the heavenly lights, who does not change like shifting shadows"* (James 1:17).

God is Holy

God is described as a holy God who is pure and sinless. The Bible tells us that *"God is light; in him there is no darkness at all"* (1 John 1:5). God commands His people to *"be holy, because I am holy"* (Leviticus 11:45).

God is Just

Another characteristic of God is that He is just. He cares about justice and He will bring His judgment. The Bible tells us that a day will come when God *"will judge the world with justice by the man he has appointed"* (Acts 17:31). We will all face the judgment of God some day, *"just as man is destined to die once, and after that to face judgment"* (Hebrews 9:27).

God is Sovereign

The Bible teaches that *"the Most High is sovereign over the kingdoms of men"* (Daniel 4:25). God is more than just a Ruler. He has absolute authority over all creation. Everything within and outside time and space is under His control. *"Yours, O LORD, is the greatness and the power and the glory and the majesty and the splendor, for everything in heaven and earth is yours. Yours, O LORD, is the kingdom; you are exalted as head over all. Wealth and honor come from you; you are the ruler of all things. In your hands are strength and power to exalt and give strength to all"* (1 Chronicles 29:11-12).

God is Truth

God is our standard of truth. He advances and confirms that which is true. He is also faithful to His promises and executes His warnings. *"Let God be true, and every man a liar"* (Romans 3:4).

God is Good

One attribute related to God's holiness is His goodness. God is good in His nature and is the source of all that is good. *"Taste and see that the LORD is good"* (Psalm 34:8).

God is Love

Another image of God is the picture of the Heavenly Father who loves His children. We are told that *"God is love. Whoever lives in love lives in God, and God in him"* (1 John 4:16). *"For God so loved the world that he gave his one and only Son, that whoever believes in him shall not perish but have eternal life"* (John 3:16).

God is Jealous

The jealousy of God is generally misunderstood. Often, jealousy in the human context is a negative trait. But the jealousy of God is a holy trait. The jealousy of God is zeal in a loving relationship. It is a zeal that protects the object of love from harm, and to avenge it when broken. This godly jealousy is a positive virtue often found in a healthy husband-wife relationship. God's love for us is so pure that anything that comes between us raises a passion in God to protect or avenge us. The jealousy of God is often revealed in the context of idolatry. *"You shall not bow down to them [idols] or worship them; for I, the LORD your God, am a jealous God..."* (Exodus 20:5)

God is Faithful

Another aspect of God's love is His faithfulness. His love is described as *"new every morning; great is your faithfulness"* (Lamentations 3:23). God's faithfulness shows that His love for us is as loyal as a mother's love towards her young.

God is Merciful

A well-known aspect of God's goodness and love is His mercy. When God is merciful to us, He does not give us the punishment that we deserve for our sins. He says, *"I will have mercy on whom I will have mercy, and I will have compassion on whom I will have compassion"* (Exodus 33:19).

God is Gracious

Just as mercy is not getting what we deserve, grace is receiving what we do not deserve. God has given us salvation and more, which no one deserves. *"For the grace of God that brings salvation has appeared to all men"* (Titus 2:11).

The Acts of God

The snapshot images of God in the Bible paint a picture of a loving and holy Being who is active in our world. The following are the things that God has done and is still doing:

He Creates

God is our Creator. He created the universe and He created mankind. *"So God created man in his own image, in the image of God he created him; male and female he created them"* (Genesis 1:27).

He Saves

God is the author of our salvation. He plans and works so that our sins can be forgiven. He tells His people: *"I, even I, am the LORD, and apart from me there is no savior"* (Isaiah 43:11).

He Reigns

The Sovereign Lord reigns and has Providence, or divine guidance, over everything. He works out every detail for His eternal purposes. *"The LORD reigns, let the nations tremble; he sits enthroned between the cherubim, let the earth shake"* (Psalm 99:1).

He Responds

God is an interactive God. He listens and responds to our prayers. God may sometimes say no to our requests, but He always responds to the voices of His children. *"Call to me and I will answer you and tell you great and unsearchable things you do not know"* (Jeremiah 33:3).

He Works

God works supernaturally in a natural world that He has created. His supernatural dealings are seen as miracles in our finite understanding. When God works in us, we experience changed lives, forgiveness, healing, and reconciliation—in other words, a miracle. The purpose of God's supernatural works is to lead us to this great salvation that He has provided. *"God also testified to it [salvation] by signs, wonders and various miracles..."* (Hebrews 2:4)

The Glory of God

When we see glimpses of who God is and some of the things that He is doing, we see God in His glory. Often when we think of "glory," we think of honour and grandeur. The glory of God in Scripture often refers to the ultimate revelation of God's being, nature, attributes, and character. Often the glory of the Lord implies the presence of God among His people.

The glory of the Lord was first mentioned when God revealed His glory to the grumbling Israelites in the desert, shown in a cloud as evidence of His presence (Exodus 16:1-10). The cloud led the Israelites to Mount Sinai where the glory of the Lord settled (Exodus 24:15-18). Moses wanted to see God's glory and got to see a portion of it (Exodus 33:12-34:35). The glory of the Lord eventually filled the tabernacle as a visual reminder of the presence of God to the Israelites during their travels. The cloud of the Lord led the Israelites by day, and the fire in the cloud led them by night (Exodus 40:34-38). When the temple of the Lord was finally built, we read that *"the glory of the Lord filled his temple"* (1 Kings 8:11).

The Israelites worshipped the Lord in the temple. However, they were also involved in idolatry. The Lord sent them prophet after prophet to warn them against their idolatry, but they refused to obey. Their sin eventually caused the glory of the Lord to leave the temple (Ezekiel 10).

Not much is said about the glory of the Lord until the time of the birth of Jesus, when an angel of the Lord appeared to the shepherds and *"the glory of the Lord shone around them, and they were terrified"* (Luke 2:9).

The Lord told the prophet Habakkuk: *"For the earth will be filled with the knowledge of the glory of the LORD, as the waters cover the sea"* (Habakkuk 2:14). Let us in our discovery of God realize that believing in a Sovereign Creator is not committing intellectual suicide. Let us discover who God is and how He wants to interact with us. Let us begin to see His glory and His presence in our lives!

11

Questions to Ponder

1. Does it take more faith *not* to believe in God?
2. How does your understanding of God compare to how He reveals Himself through the Bible?
3. What aspect of God gets your attention?
4. Since God is an interactive Being, in what supernatural way would you like to see Him work in your life?
5. Do you desire to get a glimpse of the glory of God? How much do you truly want to experience His presence?

CHAPTER TWO

Discover the Word of God

Two of the biggest ironies in history relate to the Bible. In 303 A.D., the Roman emperor Diocletian issued an edict to destroy Christians and their sacred book. Thousands of Christians died for their faith and scores of Bibles were burnt up and destroyed. However, Diocletian's edict to destroy the Bible was reversed by the next emperor, Constantine. Constantine became a Christian and twenty-five years after Diocletian's edict, he commissioned Eusebius to prepare fifty copies of the scriptures, at the expense of the government.

A French atheist, Voltaire, traveled the world speaking against the Bible. He said, "It took centuries to build up Christianity, but I'll show how one Frenchman can destroy it within 50 years." He predicted that the Bible would be reckoned an antiquated curiosity within a hundred years. Fifty years after his death, the Geneva Bible Society bought his house and printing press and proceeded to produce thousands of Bibles. His own house became the headquarters for the Geneva Bible Society. Voltaire's brilliant work is now a compilation of antiquated curiosities.

The Bible is certainly a unique book. It was written over a 1,500-year span, over forty generations. There were more than forty different authors from different walks of life: kings, political leaders, peasants, philosophers, fishermen, herdsmen, doctors, and tax collectors, to name a few. The Bible was written on three continents: Asia, Africa, and Europe. It was written at different times in different places—prisons, palaces, the wilderness—all expressing different moods. The Bible is still the all-time bestseller, the world's most widely circulated book, and is distributed in at least 1,300 languages. It is also the most loved book, and the most hated book. Men have died because of it. Emperors and kings have sought to destroy it.

Some crucial questions regarding the Bible need to be asked: Is the Bible divine revelation? Is the Bible truly "the Word of God?" In this rapidly changing age of scientific and technological advances, can we be sure that God speaks through the Bible? And if the Bible is the Word of God, what does it mean to us today? The following points about the Bible are certainly worthy of consideration.

The Evidence Showing that the Bible is the Word of God

Consider Logic

Is it logical to believe that the Bible is the Word of God? Consider what Dr. Bernard Ramm wrote about the Bible:

> No other book has been so chopped, knifed, sifted, scrutinized, and vilified. What book on philosophy or religion or psychology or *belles lettres* of classical or modern times has been subject to such a mass attack as the Bible? With such venom and skepticism? With such thoroughness and erudition? Upon every chapter, line and tenet? The Bible is still loved by millions, read by millions, and studied by millions...

It still remains the most published and most read book in the world of literature.[5]

The fact that the Bible creates so much positive and negative interest could be that the author of the Bible is God Himself. If God is an interactive God, He certainly would then want to communicate with His creation. It is not unreasonable to believe that the Sovereign Lord who creates and reigns in the universe could leave us some form of revelation. The Bible is His revelation.

On at least 2,700 occasions in the Old Testament, the prophets claimed that they were quoting God. *"Hear, O heavens! Listen, O earth! For the LORD has spoken"* (Isaiah 1:2). *"The word of the LORD came to me, saying..."* (Jeremiah 1:4). *"This is what the Sovereign LORD says..."* (Ezekiel 20:30). We must reasonably conclude that these prophets were either liars, deceivers, insane men, deceived men, or they were actually quoting God. It is not beyond logic to believe that the Bible is the Word of God.

Consider History

The Bible contains many facts of history, including details such as names, places, and dates. Such data makes the Bible historically verifiable. We can check the accuracy of the Bible against historical and scientific data outside the Bible. The historical reliability of the Bible implies that the contents of the Bible were not the imagination of any individual. In fact, the agnostic historian H. G. Wells writes:

> Almost our only sources of information about the personality of Jesus are derived from the four gospels, all of which were certainly in existence a few decades after his death. Here is a man. This part of the tale could not have been invented.[6]

---

[5] Bernard Ramm, *Protestant Christian Evidences* (Chicago: Moody, 1953), 232-33.
[6] H. G. Wells, *The Outline of History*, 420.

The historical accuracy of the Bible is significant compared to other sacred writings. Author G. B. Hardy writes in his book, *Countdown*:

> When you consider the great writings of the Egyptians, the Babylonians, the Greeks and the Romans, how they are saturated with mythology, superstition, and fantasy...replete with scientific blunders, surely it is impossible the Bible could escape without error. Still it stands without a single proven error after thirty-four centuries of scholarship.[7]

If the Bible is the Word of God, then it must speak accurately about the events and data of history. Any information in the Bible that contradicts historical fact would gives evidence that it is not revelation. The historical accuracy of the Bible proves otherwise.

Consider Archaeology

The accuracy of the Bible is mainly verified by the science of archaeology. Author Jack Cottrell writes:

> Through the wealth of data uncovered by historical and archaeological research, we are able to measure the Bible's historical accuracy. In every case where its claims can be thus tested, the Bible proves to be accurate and reliable.[8]

During the nineteenth century, many scholars saw the Bible as a book full of myths, legends, and fiction. They insisted that Moses could not have written the first five books of the Old Testament because writing had not been invented in his day. However, archaeologists have

---

[7] G. B. Hardy, *Countdown* (Chicago: Moody, 1972), 34.
[8] Jack Cottrell, *The Authority of the Bible* (Grand Rapids: Baker, 1979), 48-49.

now uncovered tablets and inscriptions that date back several hundred years before Moses.

Scholars then also claimed that John had not written the gospel of John, but that it was written some two hundred years later. However, over the past century, archaeology has uncovered a mummy in Egypt, with solid evidence dating it to around the year A.D. 100. When they began to peel away the layers of the mummy at Rylands Library in Manchester, England, they found a large fragment of the Gospel of John. It was proof that this gospel existed at the time of John, a time much earlier than the scholars claimed.

Archaeology's support for the accuracy of the Bible is overwhelming. It is shown to be true to the most obscure detail. Those who dismiss the Bible as a book of myths, legends, and fiction are ignorant of the facts of archaeology, and close their minds to the overwhelming probability that it is revelation.

Consider Prophecy

Further evidence that shows the Bible to be the Word of God is its prophecy. The Bible contains many predictions of events that were fulfilled. The fulfillment of a prophecy validates God's supernatural handprint in this world. Only God knows the future and can predict the future with extreme precision.

Many of the predictions referring to the coming Messiah in the Old Testament were fulfilled by Jesus in the New Testament. Isaiah predicted that he would be born of a virgin, which came true some seven hundred years later. Isaiah wrote: *"Therefore the Lord himself will give you a sign: The virgin will be with child and will give birth to a son, and will call him Immanuel"* (Isaiah 7:14). The prophet Micah, who lived around the same time as Isaiah, predicted that the Anointed One would be born in Bethlehem: *"But you, Bethlehem Ephrathah, though you are small among the clans of Judah, out of you will come for me one who will be ruler over Israel, whose origins are from of old, from ancient times"* (Micah 5:2). David predicted the death of the Messiah centuries before it happened. *"Dogs have surrounded me; a band of evil men has encircled me, they have pierced my hands and my feet. I can count all my bones; people stare and gloat over me. They divide my garments among them and cast lots for my clothing"* (Psalms 22:16-18).

Only God can speak of the future accurately. If the Bible is truly God's Word, then all of its predictions will come true; not a certain percentage will be fulfilled, but a hundred percent will be. *"Remember the former things, those of long ago; I am God, and there is no other; I am God, and there is none like me. I make known the end from the beginning, from ancient times, what is still to come"* (Isaiah 46:9-10).

Consider Jesus

A fifth evidence that supports the Bible as being the Word of God is the utmost respect Jesus gave the Word. Consider what Jesus said concerning the Scriptures in His day: *"Do not think that I have come to abolish the Law or the Prophets; I have not come to abolish them but to fulfill them. I tell you the truth, until heaven and earth disappear, not the smallest letter, not the least stroke of a pen, will by any means disappear from the Law until everything is accomplished"* (Matthew 5:17-18).

When Jesus was tempted by Satan in the wilderness, He used the Word of God as authority over the enemy. Jesus quoted the Old Testament and said: *"It is written: 'Man does not live on bread alone, but on every word that comes from the mouth of God'"* (Matthew 4:4).

In one of the first recorded public statements by Jesus, He went into the synagogue, took the Word of God and read from Isaiah. He read: *"The Spirit of the Lord is on me, because he has anointed me to preach good news to the poor. He has sent me to proclaim freedom for the prisoners and recovery of sight for the blind, to release the oppressed, to proclaim the year of the Lord's favour"* (Luke 4:18-19).

Jesus saw divine revelation as truth and authority. When a certain sect, the Sadducees, tried to trap Jesus because they did not believe in the resurrection, it is noteworthy how Jesus responded about the Scriptures. *"You are in error because you do not know the Scriptures or the power of God ... have you not read what God said to you, 'I am the God of Abraham, the God of Isaac, and the God of Jacob?' He is not the God of the dead but of the living"* (Matthew 22:29,31-32). If

Jesus saw the Scriptures as His authority, how can we ignore such respect for the Word of God?

The Understanding of the
Bible Being the Word of God

The Bible is the very breath of God. *"All Scripture is God-breathed and is useful for teaching, rebuking, correcting and training in righteousness, so that the man of God may be thoroughly equipped for every good work"* (2 Timothy 3:16-17). The idea of "God-breathed" means inspired by God. How does God inspire men to write down His thoughts? *"'For my thoughts are not your thoughts, neither are your ways my ways,' declares the LORD. 'As the heavens are higher than the earth, so are my ways higher than your ways and my thoughts than your thoughts'"* (Isaiah 55:8-9). There is an aspect of mystery in the process of revelation; God inspires different men in different ways.

Isaiah, for example, literally heard the words of God. *"The LORD Almighty has revealed this in my hearing"* (Isaiah 22:14). Daniel received revelation from God in a dream. *"During the night the mystery was revealed to Daniel in a vision"* (Daniel 2:19). Paul, who wrote a large portion of the New Testament, was certainly inspired. However, we are not sure of the method with which God inspired him. Paul told the Galatians: *"I want you to know, brothers, that the gospel I preached is not something that man made up. I did not receive it from any man, nor was I taught it; rather, I received it by revelation from Jesus Christ"* (Galatians 1:11-12).

We do know that God inspires men through the Holy Spirit. It is the Spirit of God who moves the men to write down what needs to be written. *"Above all, you must understand that no prophecy of Scripture came about by the prophet's own interpretation. For prophecy never had its origin in the will of man, but men spoke from God as they were carried along by the Holy Spirit"* (2 Peter 1:20-21).

Does this mean that every word in the Bible is true? This is not the necessarily the case. The Bible contains a record of historical facts and the revelation of God. Lies told in the Bible are recorded as lies. When the serpent told Eve that she would *"be like God"* (Genesis 3:5) if she ate the fruit of the tree of the knowledge of good and evil, it was recorded as a lie. The truth here is not the lie itself, but that a lie was told.

The inspiration of the Word means that the stories and accounts in the Bible are accurate. It does not mean that God approves of the words or actions of the characters in certain stories. The truth is that there are a number of stories in the Bible that are about men and women who are evil and faithless.

There are other times in the Bible when God directly speaks. The words that are from the Lord are not only accurate, but they are to be received as absolute authority. Over seven hundred times in the first five books of the Bible alone, we find the words "the Lord said." The inspired Word of God is not only accurate in the circumstances of revelation, but the words given are also true, accurate, and authoritative.

Some people see the Word of God as inspired truth. Although the Bible is inspired and true, it is more than that. Some treat the Word as two-dimensional words on a page, little more inspired than Shakespeare. However, the Word of God does not exist in just two dimensions. The Word of God is described as *"living and active. Sharper than any double-edged sword, it penetrates even to dividing soul and spirit, joints and marrow; it judges the thoughts and attitudes of the heart"* (Hebrews 4:12). Every entity that lives exists in at least three dimensions. Therefore, the Word of God must exist in at least three dimensions as well.

The Bible also tells us that *"the word of our God stands forever"* (Isaiah 40:8). *"Your word, O LORD, is eternal; it stands firm in the heavens"* (Psalm 119:89). If H. G. Wells is correct in *The Time Machine* by suggesting that the fourth dimension is time, then the eternal Word must exist in or beyond the fourth dimension. It is more accurate to say that the Word of God is a living entity that exists beyond multi-dimensions. Our relationship to the Word must be more than treating it as a body of truth to be grasped, studied, and memorized. We must interact with the Word as a living entity to be loved, cherished, and obeyed.

The Implications of the Bible Being the Word of God

Does it matter that the Bible is the Word of God? It matters tremendously, whether or not you see the Bible as inspired literature or a living entity. The Living Word must become the authority for our lives. The Bible must guide us, burn the impurities out of us, shape us, feed us, expose us, and dissect us to the position where it will grow in us. Consider the following symbols for the Word of God.

The Word is the Law

God's Word is His law. The psalmist wrote: *"All your words are true; all your righteous laws are eternal"* (Psalm 119:160). The law reveals to us our sin and guilt before the Holy God. Consider the Ten Commandments from Exodus 20:3-17.

1. "You shall have no other gods before me."
2. "You shall not make for yourself an idol in the form of anything in heaven above or on the earth beneath or in the waters below."
3. "You shall not misuse the name of the Lord your God, for the Lord will not hold anyone guiltless who misuses his name."
4. "Remember the Sabbath day by keeping it holy."
5. "Honor your father and your mother, so that you may live long in the land the Lord your God is giving you."
6. "You shall not murder."
7. "You shall not commit adultery."
8. "You shall not steal."
9. "You shall not give false testimony against your neighbor."
10. "You shall not covet…"

The law was given to show us that we are lawbreakers. *"For whoever keeps the whole law and yet stumbles at just one point is guilty of breaking all of it"* (James 2:10). We are guilty and condemned by the law. Only when we understand our sinfulness before God can we then realize our need for His mercy and grace. The Apostle Paul said that *"the law was put in charge to lead us to Christ"* (Galatians 3:24).

The Word is Our Lamp and Light

The psalmist wrote: *"Your word is a lamp to my feet and a light for my path"* (Psalm 119:105). The kinds of lamps used in the days of the psalmist were lanterns that did not give out much light. The light only illuminated the distance of a single step. However, the light was of utmost importance, especially traveling in unpredictable terrain in the dark. One wrong step could take a person to unexpected injury or death. The Word of God sheds just enough light in our lives for us to know the next step to take.

The Word is Like Fire and Hammer

"'Is not my word like fire,' declares the LORD, 'and like a hammer that breaks a rock in pieces?'" (Jeremiah 23:29). The Lord was speaking against false prophets who preached in the Lord's name but not with the Lord's message. They were preaching reckless lies and leading God's people astray. Fire can be associated with God's holiness and judgment (Deuteronomy 4:24; Zechariah 13:9). The Word is like a fire that burns up impurities in metal. It will burn up all the impurities in His people. The Word is like a hammer that shatters all those who speak contrary to Him. His Word will be His judgment.

The Word is Food

Job said: *"I have not departed from the commands of his lips; I have treasured the words of his mouth more than my daily bread"* (Job 23:12). Job saw the words of God as food for growth. The Bible is our daily spiritual food.

There are two images that relate to food concerning the Scriptures. The first image is the Word being compared to milk: *"Like newborn*

22

babies, crave pure spiritual milk, so that by it you may grow up in your salvation" (1 Peter 2:2). The second image is the Word being compared to solid food. Paul addressed the Corinthians as spiritual babies because they were not ready for solid food. He writes: *"Brothers, I could not address you as spiritual but as worldly—mere infants in Christ. I gave you milk, not solid food, for you were not yet ready for it. Indeed, you are still not ready"* (1 Corinthians 3:1-2). In Hebrews, it states: *"In fact, though by this time you ought to be teachers, you need someone to teach you the elementary truths of God's word all over again. You need milk, not solid food!"* (Hebrews 5:12). The Word of God is seen as food for our daily spiritual diet. It can be the basic teaching of milk or the deep lessons of solid food. The great challenge is to constantly feed on the Word of God.

The Word is a Mirror

James compares the Word of God to a mirror. He writes: *"Do not merely listen to the word, and so deceive yourselves. Do what it says. Anyone who listens to the word but does not do what it says is like a man who looks at his face in a mirror and, after looking at himself, goes away and immediately forgets what he looks like"* (James 1:22-24). Many people hate the Bible because they see in it their own ugliness and sinfulness. The Bible is a mirror, exposing who we are and revealing who we need to be.

The Word is a Sword

We read in the Bible, *"For the word of God is living and active. Sharper than any double-edge sword, it penetrates even to dividing soul and spirit, joints and marrow; it judges the thoughts and attitudes of the heart"* (Hebrews 4:12). The Word is described as a two-edged scalpel that is used for surgery. It acts as an instrument that cuts to our very soul and spirit in major spiritual surgery. Once the Word has dealt with us, we can use the Word as our own weapon against the enemy. *"Take the helmet of salvation and the sword of the Spirit, which is the word of God"* (Ephesians 6:17).

The Word is the Seed of Life

The Bible is seen as seed that is planted in us, producing life. *"He chose to give us birth through the word of truth, that we might be a kind of firstfruits of all he created"* (James 1:18). This Word is the seed that results in one's spiritual birth. *"For you have been born again, not of perishable seed, but of imperishable, through the living and enduring word of God"* (1 Peter 1:23).

One of the most amazing historical stories that illustrates the impact of the Bible relates to the *Mutiny on the Bounty*. Fletcher Christian, acting 2nd Lieutenant, on April 28, 1789, had more than half the ship's company joining in a mutiny against Captain Bligh and his party. The captain and his party were sent adrift, eventually reaching Timor. Fletcher Christian took the *Bounty* and the rest of the crew to Tahiti, where they had traveled previously. In September of that year, he and eight other men from the *Bounty*, six Tahitian men, eleven Tahitian women, and one child sailed away. They landed on an uninhabited island, Pitcairn's Island. The ship was burned up and they settled there.

The island at first seemed like a paradise. The men even learned how to distil liquor from one of the roots of the plants on the island. But during the next five years, the paradise became hell on earth. The men were drunk almost all the time, with many occurrences of murder, orgies, violence, and fear. After four years, only two of the fourteen men were still alive, with ten women and some children.

One of the surviving men was Alexander Smith. He discovered the Bible and a Book of Common Prayer from the remains of the *Bounty*, but he was illiterate. Edward Young, the other male survivor, was dying of consumption, but he taught Smith to read using the Bible, and died in 1801. Alexander Smith continued to read the Bible, and grew to understand it over a period of several years. Seeing the importance of teaching it to others, he began teaching the mothers and the children how to read. Through reading and obedience to the Word, Smith implemented worship and prayer.

In 1808, Captain Mayhew Folger of an American ship visited Pitcairn's Island. The members of the crew were amazed to find that thirty-five English-speaking people of Polynesian blood lived on the island, all of whom were practicing the Christian faith. British ships later visited Pitcairn's Island, finding an orderly society with no guile, alcohol, or crime. They found people who practiced love and were saturated with the Word of God.

The Bible is an amazing book. It is the inspired Word of God! We must begin to read, study, and digest it as God's revelation and authority in our lives. We must learn to interact with the Word and let it be our light, a fire and hammer to our souls, our daily food, a constant reminder of our sinfulness, and our sword in spiritual battle. We must allow the seed that came into us to grow into spiritual life and maturity. The Bible must become our life and our authority!

Questions to Ponder

1.   Does the Bible being the Word of God make sense to you? Why? Why not?

2.   Why was it important to note how Jesus treated the Word of God?

3.   Do you relate to the Word of God as a living entity or mere words on a page?

4.   What image relating to the Word of God connects with you the most?

5.   Is the Word of God the authority for your life? Why or why not?

CHAPTER THREE

Discover the Bible

One of the greatest challenges today is to understand the Bible. If it is truly a revelation from God, then it demands our understanding. The purpose of this lesson is to give an overview—a big picture of the Bible. A quick journey through the Old and New Testaments will give the traveler a good sense of where things are in the Bible.

The Two Testaments

Let us begin by taking the Bible and trying to divide it into manageable sections. We will continue to divide and sub-divide until we can digest the portions of Scripture given to us. It is common practice to focus on a certain passage of Scripture when studying the Bible. Part of the technique in Bible study is analysis, and part of analyzing a passage is dividing and sub-dividing it. Instead of starting with a few verses, or chapters, or books, we will begin with the whole Bible as our text.

The first division in the Bible is the most obvious one: the Old and New Testaments. The entire Bible contains 66 books. Approximately the first two-thirds of the Bible (39 books to be exact) make up the Old Testament. The Old Testament deals with over 4,000 years of history, mostly the history of the Israelites. The last third of the Bible (27 books) makes up the New Testament. The New Testament deals with only about 100 years of history, a very significant part of our history that focuses on Jesus Christ.

The Old Testament

The 39 books of the Old Testament can be divided into seven sub-groups. I was taught a simple way of learning the books of the Old Testament, by giving it a phone number: 593-5593. The first number 5 refers to the first five books of the Old Testament: Genesis, Exodus, Leviticus, Numbers, and Deuteronomy. These books are known as the Torah (Hebrew for 'law'). It is also called the Pentateuch, meaning five books, and they set the foundation for the entire Old Testament.

The next number, 9, refers to books in the Old Testament about pre-exilic history. The third number, 3, refers to post-exilic history in the Old Testament.

A key date to remember in Old Testament history is 586 B.C. The law told the people of God to put Him first in their lives, but they disobeyed. The children of Israel kept worshipping idols and gave their allegiance to other gods. The Lord sent them prophet after prophet to warn them, but finally they were captured by the Babylonians and taken into exile... in 586 B.C. The pre-exilic history books (Joshua, Judges, Ruth, First and Second Samuel, First and Second Kings, and First and Second Chronicles) deals with the history before the exile. The post-exilic books (Ezra, Nehemiah, and Esther) deal with the history after the exile. There are twelve history books in all of the Old Testament.

The next 5 represents the books of poetry. There are five poetic books in the Old Testament: Job, Psalms, Proverbs, Ecclesiastes, and the Song of Solomon. These poetic expressions speak to how we are to live our inner lives.

The following 5 refers to the five books in the Old Testament known as the Major Prophets. These five books speak of the basic prophecy of Isaiah, Jeremiah, Lamentations, Ezekiel, and Daniel.

Diagram 1: The Old Testament

LAW (5)		**BASIC PROPHECY (5)**
Genesis		Isaiah
Exodus		Jeremiah
Leviticus		Lamentations
Numbers		Ezekiel
Deuteronomy		Daniel
PRE-EXILIC HISTORY (9)	**POETRY (5)**	**PRE-EXILIC PROPHECY (9)**
Joshua	Job	Hosea
Judges	Psalms	Joel
Ruth	Proverbs	Amos
1-2 Samuel	Ecclesiastes	Obadiah
1-2 Kings	Song of Solomon	Jonah
1-2 Chronicles		Micah
		Nahum
		Habakkuk
		Zephaniah
POST-EXILIC HISTORY (3)		**POST-EXILIC PROPHECY (3)**
Ezra		Haggai
Nehemiah		Zechariah
Esther		Malachi

The last two numbers, 9 and 3, are what have been referred to by many as the Minor Prophets. The 9 can be seen as the pre-exilic prophets: Hosea, Joel, Amos, Obadiah, Jonah, Micah, Nahum, Habakkuk, and Zephaniah are prophets whose ministries occurred before the exile. The remaining prophets, Haggai, Zechariah, and Malachi, are seen as the post-exilic prophets because their ministries occurred afterward. Notice the beauty and symmetry that is in this library of books written by the Lord over so many years.

The Books of the Law (5)

The first five books are the books of the Law. Moses wrote these books as God inspired him. Genesis is a book full of beginnings. It speaks of the beginnings of creation, the world, and man. Genesis tells us about the fall of man and its consequences, seen in the judgments of the flood and on the tower of Babel. The book tells of the beginnings of the Israelites, God's chosen people, through the lives of its forefathers, Abraham, Isaac, Jacob, and Joseph.

Exodus begins with the Israelites as slaves in Egypt, and describes how the Israelites left Egypt through the leadership of Moses. God led the Israelites out of slavery and through many experiences in the wilderness. It was during the wilderness experience that God gave His people the Ten Commandments.

Leviticus is a book of worship that teaches God's people about worship through sacrifices. It also chronicles the journeys of the Israelites as they wandered through the wilderness.

Numbers is a book that includes an official count of the Israelites as they wandered through the wilderness.

Deuteronomy contains three sermons, each one reminding the Israelites what God had done for them, what God expected of them, and what God would do for them. It is a second law to God's people, reminding them to be holy and obedient to the Lord as a way of life.

Diagram 2: Books of the Law

GENESIS	• Beginnings of creation, fall, flood, and nations. • Beginnings of Israel through Abraham, Isaac, Jacob, and Joseph.
EXODUS	• Moses leads Israel out of Egypt.
LEVITICUS	• Worship God through sacrifices and feasts.
NUMBERS	• The number of Israelites wandering in the wilderness.
DEUTERONOMY	• The second law on obedience and holiness.

The Books of Pre-exilic History (9)

The next nine books of the Old Testament cover pre-exilic history. They span over eight hundred years of Israelite history (1405-586 B.C.). These history books can be subdivided into two sections. The first division contains the theocratic books (Joshua, Judges, and Ruth), when Israel was a nation ruled directly by God (a theocracy). The second division contains the monarchical books (Samuel, Kings, and Chronicles), when the Israelites were ruled by kings.

The book of Joshua is about God using Joshua to conquer the land of Canaan. Judges differs from Joshua, as a book, in that it focuses on defeat, as opposed to the conquest and victory that occurred earlier. God allowed His people to be oppressed because of their sins. A judge is a deliverer whom God raised to deliver Israel out of an oppressor's hand after His people repented from their sins. Ruth is a beautiful love story about a Moabite widow who became the great-grandmother of David.

Diagram 3: Books of Pre-Exilic History

JOSHUA	• Joshua conquers Canaan.
JUDGES	• Defeated Israel is delivered by judges.
RUTH	• A love story of Ruth and Boaz.
1 SAMUEL	• The decline of judges and the rise of kings.
2 SAMUEL	• David's reign in Hebron and Jerusalem.
1 KINGS	• Solomon and the divided kingdom.
2 KINGS	• The fall of the kingdoms of Israel and Judah.
1 CHRONICLES	• The life and reign of David.
2 CHRONICLES	• The lives and reigns of Solomon and the kings of Judah.

First Samuel gives account for the decline in judges, following the lives of Eli and Samuel while showing the rise of kings through the lives of King Saul and King David. Second Samuel tells the story of

David's reign in Hebron and Jerusalem. First Kings tells us about Solomon and the divided kingdom that came after him. The Israelites were divided into two kingdoms: Israel in the north and Judah in the south. Second Kings takes us through the fall of the northern kingdom, Israel, by the Assyrians and the fall of the southern kingdom, Judah, at the hands of the Babylonians. First Chronicles covers the life and reign of David while Second Chronicles covers the life and reigns of Solomon and the kings of Judah.

The Books of Post-Exilic History (3)

The next three books of the Old Testament are books of post-exilic history (Ezra, Nehemiah, and Esther). These are restoration books, depicting a time when a remnant of the Jews returned to their homeland after seventy years of captivity in Babylon.

Ezra is a book about restoring the temple and people of God through the leadership of Zerubbabel and Ezra. Nehemiah tells the story about a cupbearer of a Persian king who helped rebuild the walls of Jerusalem. Esther is a lovely story about a Jewish girl who became queen of Persia and helped save her people from annihilation.

Diagram 4: Books of Post-Exilic History

EZRA	• Restoring the temple of God and the people of God.
NEHEMIAH	• Rebuilding the walls of Jerusalem.
ESTHER	• A Jewish girl who becomes a Persian queen.

The Books of Poetry (5)

The next five books in the Old Testament are considered poetic books: Job, Psalms, Proverbs, Ecclesiastes, and the Song of Solomon.

The book of Job teaches us about God's control in the midst of human suffering. Psalms is a collection of songs often sung in worship. Proverbs is a collection of wise sayings, mostly given by Solomon. Ecclesiastes is another book by Solomon reflecting on the meaning of life. The Song of Solomon, also known as the Song of Songs, is about the wooing and marriage of a shepherdess by a king. Solomon saturated this love song with romantic love.

Diagram 5: Books of Poetry

JOB	• God is in control in the midst of suffering.
PSALMS	• A collection of worship songs to the Lord.
PROVERBS	• A collection of wise sayings for life.
ECCLESIASTES	• Solomon's reflection on the purpose of life.
SONG OF SOLOMON	• A love song about a shepherdess and a king.

The Books of Basic Prophecy (5)

The next five books are known as the Major Prophets, and they contain basic prophecy. These books are Isaiah, Jeremiah, Lamentations, Ezekiel, and Daniel. They are generally longer than the rest of the prophetic books. A prophet was a servant of the Lord called to proclaim the message of God. They often told what the Lord had revealed to him or her concerning the past, present, or future.

Diagram 6: Books of Basic Prophecy

ISAIAH	• Isaiah speaks on the judgment and glory of God.
JEREMIAH	• Jeremiah speaks out against the spiritual and moral decay of Judah.
LAMENTATIONS	• The laments of Jeremiah after the fall of Jerusalem.
EZEKIEL	• Ezekiel gives hope to a spiritually dead Judah.
DANIEL	• Daniel, the man of prayer and interpreter of dreams.

The book of Isaiah speaks much about the judgment of God and ends with hope for the glory of God. The book of Jeremiah addresses the spiritual and moral decay of Judah and speaks of God's judgment against it. Lamentations is a book of laments by Jeremiah after the fall of Jerusalem. Ezekiel is a book that uses the imagery of dry bones to symbolize Judah's spiritually lifeless condition. It also gives hope for the restoration of Israel someday. Daniel is a book full of dreams and visions relevant to our history and our future.

The Books of Pre-Exilic Prophecy (9)

The next nine Old Testament books contain prophecy given before the exile in 586 B.C. These books are Hosea, Joel, Amos, Obadiah, Jonah, Micah, Nahum, Habakkuk, and Zephaniah.

Diagram 7: Books of Pre-Exilic Prophecy

HOSEA	• The faithfulness of God to adulterous Israel.
JOEL	• A warning to Judah of the army of locusts who will clean their land.
AMOS	• Israel does not measure up to God's plumb-line of righteousness.
OBADIAH	• The destruction of Edom and the deliverance of Israel.
JONAH	• God's mercy to the Ninevites through Jonah.
MICAH	• There will be justice when surrounded by injustice.
NAHUM	• Nineveh will be flooded with an army of destruction.
HABAKKUK	• Habakkuk questions God and ends up praising Him.
ZEPHANIAH	• The Day of the Lord is coming.

Hosea is a book that compares an adulterous Israel to a faithful Lord. The book of Joel predicts an army from the north, which will come like a plague of locusts to pick Judah clean unless the people there repent. The book of Amos speaks against hypocrisy and spiritual indifference in prosperous Israel. Obadiah is a book that predicts the destruction of Edom and the deliverance of Israel.

Jonah was a prophet who was swallowed by a great fish after he avoided preaching to the Ninevites. The book teaches about God's mercy to repentive Gentile nations. Micah speaks on justice to a society full of injustice. Nahum tells of the destruction of the city of Nineveh at the hands of an army who was to enter their city like a flood. Habakkuk questions God and concludes with praise for Him. Zephaniah proclaims the coming Day of the Lord in Judah and ends with a promise of restoration.

The Books of Post-Exilic Prophecy (3)

The remaining three books of the Old Testament are prophecies given after the exile in 586 B.C. Haggai exhorts the people of God to rebuild the temple of God and receive the blessing of God. Zechariah was a priest who also encouraged the people to continue the rebuilding of the temple of God, with a prediction that the Messiah's glory would one day dwell in it. Malachi is the last book of the Old Testament, and speaks against the Israelites, who had unfaithful hearts towards the Lord. The Old Testament ends with a prediction of the coming of the Lord. The people of God had learned very little from their captivity, committing the same kinds of sins that had resulted in their exile.

Diagram 8: Books of Post-Exilic Prophecy

HAGGAI	• A call to rebuild the temple of God.
ZECHARIAH	• Encouragement to rebuild the temple for the Messiah.
MALACHI	• Malachi speaks of Israel's unfaithfulness and the Lord's coming.

The New Testament

Four hundred years pass between the close of the Old Testament and the beginning of the New Testament. The Old Testament centered mainly on God's relationship with the children of Israel, always emphasizing the promise of a coming Messiah. The New Testament is all about that Messiah (Anointed One). The Messiah is *the Lamb of God, who takes away the sin of the world!* (John 1:29). The New Testament is all about Jesus Christ.

Diagram 9: The New Testament

HISTORY (5)		LETTER TO JEWISH BELIEVERS (1)
Matthew		Hebrews
Mark		
Luke		
John		
Acts		
LETTERS TO CHURCHES (9)		**LETTERS FROM PASTORS (3)**
Romans	**LETTER TO INDIVIDUAL (1)**	James
1-2 Corinthians		1-2 Peter
Galatians	Philemon	
Ephesians		
Philippians		
Colossians		
1-2 Thessalonians		
LETTERS TO PASTORS (3)		**LETTERS FROM ELDERS (5)**
1-2 Timothy		1-3 John
Titus		Jude
		Revelation

The 27 books of the New Testament can easily be remembered with another phone number: 593-1135. Consider the fact that the New

Testament is built from the Old Testament. It therefore has a similar code (593).

The New Testament number will have the same start as the Old Testament. The first number, 5, refers to the five books of history in the New Testament. The first four books are known as the gospels: Matthew, Mark, Luke, and John. The fifth book is Acts, which deals with the ascension of Jesus and early church history. The rest of the New Testament is comprised of letters.

The Apostle Paul wrote at least thirteen of the New Testament letters, each of them dealing with living a life that is "in Christ." The 9 represents nine letters that Paul wrote to churches in various cities: Romans, First Corinthians, Second Corinthians, Galatians, Ephesians, Philippians, Colossians, First Thessalonians, and Second Thessalonians.

The next number, a 3, is associated with pastors. The Old Testament has prophets and the New Testament has pastors. Paul wrote three letters to two pastors: First Timothy, Second Timothy, and Titus.

The last letter of Paul is associated with the fourth number, 1, which was sent to an individual named Philemon.

The last nine books of the New Testaments are letters of encouragement for believers to persevere in their faith. The fifth number, another 1, refers to Hebrews, which was written to encourage Jewish believers to persevere in their faith. The 3 represents letters written by two pastors: James, First Peter, and Second Peter. The final 5 refers to First John, Second John, Third John, Jude, and Revelation, which are letters by two elders to encourage believers to persevere in the last days.

The Books of History (5)

The first five books of the New Testament are documents of history beginning with the four gospels, or the Good News. These books are all about Jesus Christ. There are four accounts of Jesus' life: Matthew, Mark, Luke, and John. Each of the gospels reveals the life and ministry of Jesus, ending with accounts of His death and resurrection. Each also emphasizes a different aspect of Jesus' life. It is like four different newspapers covering the same event, and coming up with stories that are both similar and different.

Matthew wrote for the Jewish mind, affirming Jesus to be the Messiah and King. Mark presented Jesus as a humble servant of man who did not come *"to be served, but to serve"* (Mark 10:45, NIC). Luke was a doctor who presented Jesus as the "Son of Man," emphasizing his perfect humanity. John presented Jesus as the "Son of God," revealing His deity.

The other book of history is Acts, which concerns the ministry of the Holy Spirit in the early church, after Jesus ascended into heaven. The book follows the early ministries of the Apostle Peter and the Apostle Paul. Acts follows the church, beginning with the Jews in Jerusalem, then covering the Jews and Samaritans in Judea and Samaria, and finally to the Gentiles in the ends of the earth.

Diagram 10: Books of History

MATTHEW	• Jesus is the King of kings.
MARK	• Jesus is the Servant of Man.
LUKE	• Jesus is the Son of Man.
JOHN	• Jesus is the Son of God.
ACTS	• The ministry of the Holy Spirit in the early Church.

The Letters of Paul to the Churches (9)

The Apostle Paul wrote nearly half the books in the New Testament. The writings of Paul are presented in the form of letters written to churches, pastors, and to a lay individual. We learn much about the early church and their teachings through these God-inspired by God.

Paul wrote nine letters to Christians in the cities of Rome, Corinth, Galatia, Ephesus, Philippi, Colossae, and Thessalonica. Each book presents unique teachings about living the Christian faith "in Christ." The Book of Romans teaches how we can have the righteousness of God, since our debt of sin has been paid in full. Paul wrote two letters to the believers in Corinth. The first letter, First Corinthians, addressed the problems the Corinthian church was struggling with at the time.

The second letter, Second Corinthians, was Paul's response to the false teachers of the day who were questioning his credentials and authority as an apostle.

Diagram 11: Letters of Paul to Churches

ROMANS	• The righteousness of God.
1 CORINTHIANS	• The problems in the church.
2 CORINTHIANS	• Paul's apostolic credentials and authority.
GALATIANS	• Our freedom in Christ.
EPHESIANS	• Our belief and our behaviour in Christian living.
PHILIPPIANS	• Our joy being in Christ.
COLOSSIANS	• Christ is supreme in our lives.
1 THESSALONIANS	• Excel in faith, because Christ is coming.
2 THESSALONIANS	• Stand firm and work until Christ comes.

Galatians is about the freedom believers have in Christ. Ephesians talks about living the Christian life in both our belief and behaviour. Philippians tells us about the joy believers have in Christ. Colossians is all about Christ and our relationship with Him.

Paul also wrote two letters to what was a model church in Thessalonica. First Thessalonians was a letter that encouraged the believers to excel in their faith because Christ was coming. Second Thessalonians responds to the false teaching that Christ had already come. Paul encouraged the believers to stand firm in the faith and work hard until Christ comes.

The Letters of Paul to the Pastors (3)

Paul wrote three letters to the pastors Timothy and Titus, and so they are known also as the Pastoral Epistles. These books are letters of encouragement on leadership matters. The first letter to Timothy, First Timothy, encourages the young man in his pastoral leadership. The second letter to him, Second Timothy, is considered to have been Paul's final letter, containing words of wisdom and encouragement to Timothy before his death. Titus was also a young minister receiving pastoral advice from Paul on church leadership.

Diagram 12: Letters of Paul to Pastors

1 TIMOTHY	• Timothy learns about pastoral leadership.
2 TIMOTHY	• Paul's final words of wisdom and encouragement.
TITUS	• Pastoral wisdom on church leadership.

The Letter of Paul to an Individual (1)

At the centre of this New Testament phone number is the book of Philemon. Philemon is a letter that Paul wrote asking the man, who was a slave owner, to forgive his runaway slave. In the midst of all the letters about being "in Christ," this simple letter reveals the full understanding of every good thing we have in Him.

Diagram 13: Letter of Paul to an Individual

PHILEMON	• Paul encourages Philemon to forgive Onesimus.

Encouraging Letters to Jewish Believers (1)

The last nine books of the New Testament are letters to encourage believers to persevere in the faith. Hebrews is a letter by an unidentified author, revealing the superiority and sufficiency of Jesus Christ over any empty religion. It was written to encourage Jewish believers who were waning in their faith.

Diagram 14: Encouraging Letter to Jewish Believers

HEBREWS	• Christ is superior and sufficient.

Encouraging Letters From Pastors (3)

The next three New Testament letters were written by the first two pastors in the church in Jerusalem, James and Peter. Just as there were three letters written to pastors, here there are three letters written by pastors. These letters were written to encourage believers to persevere in the midst of difficulties. James, a half-brother of Jesus, did not believe in Christ until after the resurrection. His letter is a practical approach to the Christian faith.

Peter wrote two letters to the Christian community. The first, First Peter, was written to encourage believers to continue living for God, knowing that their suffering had a purpose. The second letter, Second Peter, was a warning against false teachers in the church, and urged believers to be on their guard until Christ comes.

Diagram 15: Encouraging Letters From Pastors

JAMES	• Practical Christian living.
1 PETER	• Continue to suffer for God's purpose.
2 PETER	• Beware of false teachers among you.

Encouraging Letters from Elders (5)

The final five letters of the New Testament were written by two elders of the church in order to encourage believers to persevere in the faith during the last days. John was also concerned about false teachers of his day and addressed the issue in his first letter. First John is about having true fellowship and assurance of salvation in the midst of false teachings. Second John is an encouragement to walk in truth and love, though it reiterated the importance of believers not welcoming false teachers. Third John is a personal letter from the Apostle John to Gaius, encouraging him to continue showing hospitality to Christian strangers.

Jude was another half-brother of Jesus, who warned believers of the godless among them and encouraged them to contend for the faith. The last book in the Bible is Revelation, a book describing a vision given to John by Jesus about events in the last days.

Diagram 16: Encouraging Letters From Elders

1 JOHN	• True fellowship and assurance.
2 JOHN	• Walk in truth and love.
3 JOHN	• John encourages Gaius to continue to show hospitality.
JUDE	• Contend for the faith.
REVELATION	• Future events in the last days.

A good way to remember the number of books in the New Testament (27) is to take the number of books in the Old Testament (39) and multiply its two digits (3 x 9 = 27). A good way to remember the New Testament phone number is to multiply the first three numbers (the area code) to receive the last three digits (5 x 9 x 3 = 135).

The Big Picture

What is the big picture of the Bible? If we start in Genesis, we find that God created man in his own image. However, man disobeyed God and was driven out of the Garden of Eden, becoming increasing wicked. Man became so wicked that God judged the earth with a flood, leaving only Noah and his family left. Noah's descendents began to repopulate the earth until there were many people groups. God chose a man named Abram to follow after the Lord to a promised land. Abram become Abraham, the father of many nations. God was to be Abraham's God and the God of the descendents after him. Abraham's son was Isaac, who had two sons named Esau and Jacob. God changed Jacob's name, which meant 'deceiver,' to Israel, meaning 'he struggled with God.' The children of Israel became the chosen people who struggled with God.

The Old Testament follows the spiritual journey of the Israelites in their struggle with God. God gave them the Ten Commandments and told them never to worship any idols. Throughout their journey, however, they struggled to be faithful to God. Even after they reached the promised land with Joshua, the Israelites continued to be unfaithful.

They wanted a king like all the other nations surrounding them, and so God gave them King Saul.

After the reigns of King David and King Solomon, the children of Israel were divided into two kingdoms: Israel in the north and Judah in the south. The chosen people of God continued through these times to chase after other gods and idols. The Lord sent them prophet after prophet, but they did not repent. Finally, the Lord allowed them to be destroyed and taken to Babylon for seventy years. It is interesting that after the Israelites returned from exile, we do not read much about them chasing after idols again.

A theme at the heart of Israel's history is the expectation of a coming Messiah, the Anointed One, who was expected to save the people of God. The Old Testament points to the Messiah, and the New Testament is all about the arrival of the Messiah (Christ), in the person of Jesus. The Bible is all about Jesus: His life, His death, His resurrection, and His significance in our lives.

Questions to Ponder

1. Have you ever found the Bible difficult to understand? Why?
2. What aspect(s) of the Old Testament fascinate you today?
3. What aspect(s) of the New Testament fascinate you today?
4. How does understanding the big picture of the Bible help you to understand it better?
5. What question(s) have you always wanted to ask about the Bible?

CHAPTER FOUR

Discover Jesus

The core of Christianity centers on Jesus Christ. The Old Testament points expectantly to a coming Messiah. The New Testament is all about that Messiah (Christ), named Jesus. Gandhi said, "I tell the Hindus that their lives will be imperfect if they do not also study reverently the teaching of Jesus."[9] Lord Byron said, "If ever God was man or man was God, Jesus Christ was both."[10] To discover Jesus is to discover what the whole Christian faith is all about. Christianity is a love relationship with Jesus Christ.

The Existence of Jesus

A case could easily be made revealing Jesus Christ as the focal point of history. Many distinguished scholars have affirmed the historicity of

---

[9] Steve Kumar, *Christianity for Skeptics*. (Peabody, Massachusetts: Hendrickson Publishers, Inc., 2000), 82

Christ. H. G. Wells, the famous writer and agnostic, writes concerning Jesus: "Here was a man. This part of the tale could not have been invented."[11] It is impossible to believe in Jesus Christ apart from His history. Writer Michael Green writes: "Once disprove the historicity of Jesus Christ, and Christianity will collapse like a pack of cards."[12] To diminish the existence of Jesus to some myth is to ignore centuries of scholarship and historical evidences that are before us.

The Birth of Jesus

Every Christmas, Christians around the world celebrate the birth of Jesus. What was unique about the birth was that Jesus was born of a virgin, thus fulfilling Old Testament prophecy. About seven hundred years earlier, the prophet Isaiah wrote: *"Therefore the Lord himself will give you a sign: The virgin will be with child and will give birth to a son, and will call him Immanuel"* (Isaiah 7:14). Around the same time, another prophet, named Micah, predicted the birthplace of the Messiah. He wrote: *"But you, Bethlehem Ephrathah, though you are small among the clans of Judah, out of you will come for me one who will be ruler over Israel, whose origins are from of old, from ancient times"* (Micah 5:2).

The virgin birth of Jesus was a not a natural likelihood, but it was a supernatural possibility. If His birth was a normal birth, then Jesus would have been just another special human being. The fact that the Virgin Mary conceived via the Holy Spirit made Him a very unique child. Even Joseph, who was at the time engaged to Mary, had a hard time accepting Mary's pregnancy as being supernatural. However Joseph did respond positively when an angel told him, *"Joseph son of David, do not be afraid to take Mary home as your wife, because what is conceived in her is from the Holy Spirit. She will give birth to a son, and you are to give him the name Jesus, because he will save his people*

---

[10] Ibid.
[11] H.G. Wells, *The Outline of History*, 1.420.
[12] Michael Green, *Runaway World*. (London: InterVarsity Press, 1968), 2.

from their sins" (Matthew 1:20-21). The virgin birth made it possible for Jesus to be both God and man. It was the means through which God could supernaturally become man.

Some time after Jesus was born, Magi (or Wise Men) from the east came to Jerusalem in search of the one born king of the Jews. The Magi in ancient times were known as kingmakers. Historically, no Persian could be king until they had mastered the scientific and religious disciplines of the Magi. The Magis' influence and power continued in the Greek and Roman empires, where we encounter this one sect with strong Jewish influence. When Jesus was born, the Magi came and worshipped Him as king.

The Life of Jesus

After the visit of the Magi, Joseph took Jesus and his family to Egypt to flee from the evils of King Herod. The family eventually settled in Nazareth, where Jesus grew up. Other than on one occasion—at age twelve, when Jesus amazed everyone in the temple courts in Jerusalem with his understanding and debates with the wise men of the day— Jesus lived in obscurity for some thirty years.

The next time we hear about Jesus is when He began His public ministry. John the Baptist introduced the public to Jesus when he baptized Him. Afterward, the Spirit led Jesus into the desert, where He was tempted by the devil. After forty days in the wilderness, Jesus went throughout Galilee preaching the message of the kingdom and healing the sick. His first of many miracles was performed at a wedding in Cana, where He turned water into wine.

Jesus cleansed the temple of God in his first recorded visit to Jerusalem after the start of His public ministry. It was at that time that He interacted with a variety of people, from a religious leader like Nicodemus to the lowly in society like the Samaritan woman. Jesus was open and accepting of all people, no matter who they were in society. He was severely criticized for socializing with "sinners" and those who were seen as the bottom feeders of society.

Much of Jesus' ministry was in Galilee. He used Capernaum as His home base. The ministry of Jesus included many miracles by which the blind received sight, the lame walked, those with leprosy were cured, the deaf heard, and the dead were raised. Jesus also preached the good news to the poor and taught great truths through many parables. At the same time, Jesus spent His three years mentoring twelve disciples, who would all desert Him in His time of need.

Jesus eventually traveled to Jerusalem via Perea, ministering as He went. The three years of Jesus' ministry concluded with His final days in Jerusalem, beginning with his triumphal entry into the city on a donkey. It was an entry where crowds of people spread their cloaks and branches on the road to honour Jesus as their king. Jesus fulfilled the prophecy of Zechariah, who had written some five hundred years earlier: *"Rejoice greatly, O Daughter of Zion! Shout, Daughter of Jerusalem! See, your king comes to you, righteous and having salvation, gentle and riding on a donkey, on a colt, the foal of a donkey"* (Zechariah 9:9).

After Jesus' dramatic entry into Jerusalem, it was recorded that He again entered the temple and cleansed it. He continued to teach His disciples while being challenged by the religious leaders of the day. Later that week, Jesus and His disciples observed the Jewish Passover, known today as the Last Supper. It was at this feast that Jesus took the bread and the cup and told his disciples of His coming death and the one who would betray Him. After praying in the Garden of Gethsemane, Jesus was arrested and taken away.

Jesus was taken and tried before both religious and political leaders. He was unfairly condemned to death, being guilty of nothing. Jesus was crucified on the cross and died an innocent man. However, His death was significant because of His holy life. John the Baptist understood that Jesus was a kind of sacrifice for the sins of mankind when he pointed to Jesus and said: *"Look, the Lamb of God, who takes away the sin of the world!"* (John 1:29).

Jesus' life was full of acts of kindness, love, mercy, and grace. His selfless teachings astounded scholars, pierced the hearts of hypocrites, and comforted the humbled. Jesus not only changed the face of history, He was and is history. His life made an impact that has eternal consequences. Will Durant, an agnostic and former professor at Columbia University, wrote concerning Jesus: "That a few simple men should in one generation have invented so powerful and appealing a personality, so lofty an ethic, and so inspiring a vision of human brotherhood, would be a miracle far more incredible than any recorded in the gospels." [13]

The Death of Jesus

The holy life of Jesus should not have resulted in His death as a common criminal. However, Jesus' death on the cross was the most recorded and analyzed death in history. Those who were closest to Jesus did not hesitate to point out that He was sinless. John wrote, *"...and in him is no sin"* (1 John 3:5). Peter quoted Isaiah in reference to Christ, saying, *"He committed no sin, and no deceit was found in his mouth"* (1 Peter 2:22). Even the enemies of Christ admitted His perfection in life. Judas, who betrayed Jesus, was filled with remorse, saying, *"I have sinned ... for I have betrayed innocent blood"* (Matthew 27:4). A statement from some of those who were responsible for Jesus' death testified: *"Surely he was the Son of God!"* (Matthew 27:54) To admit that Jesus was the Son of God was to admit that He was as sinless as God was. Even Pilate admitted that Jesus was an *"innocent man"* (Matthew 27:19) who did not deserve to die.

After Jesus was arrested in the Garden of Gethsemane, He stood for trial six separate times. The first trial was before Annas, the father-in-law of Caiaphas, and took place immediately after the arrest of Jesus (John 18:12-24). This trial was illegal, taking place at night, contrary to Jewish law. There were no indictments prepared, no witnesses heard, and no counsel was provided for the defendant. The officials physically abused Jesus when they disagreed with His responses to the questions He was given. Jesus was then immediately brought before Caiaphas, who also tried Him (Matthew 26:57-68; Mark 14:53-65). False

---

[13] Will Durant, "Caesar and Christ," in *The Story of Civilization* (New York: Simon & Schuster, 1944), 3.557.

witnesses were produced at this trial and Jesus was convicted after he affirmed that He was indeed the Christ. It was recorded that at this trial the religious leaders *"spit in his face and struck him with their fists. Others slapped him and said, 'Prophesy to us, Christ. Who hit you?'"* (Matthew 26:67-68)

A third trial was held in the morning, at which Jesus was convicted of blasphemy for claiming to be the Son of God (Matthew 27:1-2; Mark 15:1; Luke 22:66-71). He was then sent to the Roman governor, Pilate, where Jesus was accused of perverting the nation by opposing payment of taxes to Caesar, and claiming to be the King of the Jews. The fourth trial before Pilate was brief since Pilate learned that Jesus was from Galilee and was therefore under Herod's jurisdiction. Pilate sent Jesus to Herod, who was in Jerusalem at the time. It was at this trial (Luke 23:8-12) that Jesus was mocked and ridiculed by Herod and his soldiers before being returned to Pilate.

The final trial before Pilate was a travesty of justice. Pilate tried to acquit Jesus and offered to scourge and release Him (Matthew 27:15-26; Mark 15:6-15; Luke 23:18-25; John 18:29-19:16). However, the chief priests and their officials wanted Jesus crucified. Pilate offered them a choice to free Jesus or a known rebel and murderer named Barabbas. They chose to crucify Jesus and release Barabbas. Pilate eventually pronounced the death sentence on Jesus, according to the will of the people. It was at this trial that Pilate had Jesus flogged, a beating so severe that it would have left a typical person barely alive. The soldiers also gave Jesus a crown of thorns, pressed down mockingly into His brow.

Jesus had to carry His own cross until He was too weak from the beating to bear it further. Simon of Cyrene was there and took over for Jesus in carrying the cross to Golgotha ('the Place of the Skull'). It was on that hill where Jesus was crucified with two other criminals. Jesus was nailed to the cross He had earlier carried. An inscription was written and fastened to the cross that read: "Jesus of Nazareth, the King of the Jews." As Jesus hung on the cross at the peak of the day, darkness came over all the land. When He gave up His spirit, the curtain of the temple was torn into two from top to bottom and the earth shook. Jesus lived like no one ever lived, and died like no one has ever died.

Why was it necessary for Jesus to die? Why did He have to die to become our Saviour? In Greek mythology, when Paris abducted Helen of Troy, Agamemnon was put at the head of the expedition to Troy to take back his brother's wife. When the Greek fleet set sail from Aulis, they encountered no winds. They discovered that the reason for the lack of wind was that the goddess Artemis was angry with them for the lack of respect they had shown her. Artemis demanded that Agamemnon sacrifice his daughter Iphigenia in order to appease her wrath. When Agamemnon finally sacrificed his daughter, the wrath of Artemis was appeased and he was allowed to sail to Troy.

Our God is so holy that His reaction to any sin is wrath. Old Testament priests often offered sacrifices to appease or atone for sins. Jesus is *"the Lamb of God, who takes away the sin of the world!"* (John 1:29) Some suggest that God could have just snapped His fingers and the world would be all right. Although God has the power to do so, it is not within His nature to do so. His holy nature would never compromise with sin. His holy nature requires Him to react and deal with sin in a godly manner.

The death of Christ was God's sacrifice for our sins. Instead of man making the sacrifices to appease His wrath, God made the sacrifice for man. Jesus *"is the atoning sacrifice for our sins, and not only for ours but also for the sins of the whole world"* (1 John 2:2). The death of Jesus satisfied the wrath of God. The penalty was severe. It shows us how serious God views sin. It also shows us how much God loves us in responding to sin in the way He did. *"But God demonstrates his own love for us in this: While we were still sinners, Christ died for us"* (Romans 5:8).

At the core of the message of Christianity is that Jesus died for our sins. To understand this concept is to understand the concept of debt. The Bible tells us that *"the wages of sin is death, but the gift of God is eternal life in Christ Jesus our Lord"* (Romans 6:23). Our sins put us in great debt before our Heavenly Father. We deserve death as a result of our sins. It is like a beggar owing a king billions of dollars with no way of paying it. But the king in this story sacrifices his own Son in order to pay off the beggar's debt. The king not only forgives the debt, but he gives the beggar millions of dollars in exchange. The beggar no longer lives as a beggar, but as a rich man.

When we were in the debt of sin, the Father saw us as sinners, each one of us deserving of death. However, Jesus died for our sins and took our punishment. *"But he was pierced for our transgressions, he was crushed for our iniquities; the punishment that brought us peace was upon him, and by his wounds we are healed. We all, like sheep, have gone astray, each of us has turned to his own way; and the LORD has laid on him the iniquity of us all"* (Isaiah 53:5-6). Jesus died as our substitute. He died in our place. *"For Christ died for sins once for all, the righteous for the unrighteous, to bring you to God. He was put to death in the body but made alive by the Spirit"* (1 Peter 3:18).

When we believe that Jesus died for our sins, we receive Him as we receive any gift. *"Yet to all who received him, to those who believed in his name, he gave the right to become children of God"* (John 1:12). The Father no longer sees us as sinners, but as His children, with the righteousness of Christ. *"For just as through the disobedience of the one man the many were made sinners, so also through the obedience of the one man the many will be made righteous"* (Romans 5:19).

The Resurrection of Jesus

The other core message of Christianity is that Jesus rose from the dead. After Jesus died, His body was taken and buried in a tomb owned by Joseph of Arimathea. With so many rumours of Jesus' disciples' attempts to steal the body of Jesus, the Pharisees persuaded Pilate to have the tomb sealed and watched by Roman guards. This was recorded to show that Jesus did miraculously rise from the dead in the midst of great opposition.

It was on that Sunday morning, when Mary Magdalene and the other Mary, the mother of James, went to look at the tomb and found it empty. An angel appeared to them and proclaimed: *"Do not be afraid, for I know that you are looking for Jesus, who was crucified. He is not here; he has risen, just as he said. Come and see the place where he lay"* (Matthew 28:5-6). The women were overjoyed and quickly shared the news with the disciples. Eventually, Jesus appeared to His disciples in the flesh, visiting them several times, teaching and comforting them. Jesus stayed forty days on the earth after the resurrection before ascending into heaven.

How certain can we be about the resurrection of Jesus? The scholar James Edwin Orr writes: "No single example can be produced of belief in the resurrection of an historical personage such as Jesus was: none at least on which anything was ever founded ... the Christian resurrection is thus a fact without historical analogy."[14] The evidence for the resurrection of Christ is too overwhelming to ignore.

The Reality of Church

The Christian church started in A.D. 32 (Anno Domini, in the year of our Lord) in Jerusalem. The disciples of Jesus were mostly hiding, afraid, and in fear for their lives after the death of Christ. What made these cowardly disciples stand boldly before the people of Jerusalem only weeks later and preach messages that would turn the world upside down? It was the fact that Jesus rose from the dead that changed their hearts and attitudes, giving them the boldness to proclaim the truth. The disciples started what is now known as the church. The existence of the church today gives evidence that Jesus did rise from the dead.

The Reality of Sunday

The first day of the week is Sunday. Jesus rose from the dead on the first day of the week (Matthew 28:1). Christians in the early church met on the first day of the week (Acts 20:7). What changed the large Jewish population from worshipping on the Sabbath (Saturday) to worshipping on a Sunday? The fact that many churches today worship on Sunday gives evidence that Jesus did rise from the dead on the first day of the week.

---

[14] James Edwin Orr, *The Resurrection of Jesus* (Joplin: College Press, 1972) 224.

The Reality of Witnesses

There were many witnesses who saw Jesus after his death. All the gospel writers and disciples were witnesses to His resurrection. Paul tells us that there was a time when over five hundred people saw Jesus at once (1 Corinthians 15:6). This eliminates any possibilities of some kind of hallucination could explain it. The most credible witness was Thomas, who doubted Jesus rose from the dead. When Jesus did appear to Thomas, He asked Thomas to touch His hands, where the nails had been, and to touch His side where He had been pierced by a spear. Thomas said to Jesus: *"'My Lord and my God!' Then Jesus told him, 'Because you have seen me, you have believed; blessed are those who have not seen and yet have believed'"* (John 20:28-29).

The Reality of the Empty Tomb

If He did not rise from the dead, where was His body? Sceptics have suggested that the women went to the wrong tomb. If the women went to the wrong tomb, though, it would be very easy for the enemies of Jesus to point out the right tomb. The fact that the chief priests tried to bribe the Roman guards to lie about the body being stolen (Matthew 28:11-15) meant that the women did go to the right tomb.

The possibility that the disciples stole the body is inconsistent with their lives. The disciples were cowards who ran away at the first sign of trouble. Even if they attempted to steal the body, it would have been difficult for them to get by the Roman guards and remove the sealed stone. Eventually, every one of the disciples died convinced that Jesus rose from the dead. If they did steal the body, not many of them would die for a lie. Jesus did come out of the tomb supernaturally, not naturally.

The Reality of the Written Word

All of the New Testament writers viewed the resurrection as an accepted event. Matthew, Mark, Luke, and John all recorded the resurrection as a historical fact. Peter told the crowd in Jerusalem that *"God has raised this Jesus to life, and we are all witnesses of the fact"* (Acts 2:32). The Apostle Paul wrote: *"Christ has indeed been raised from the dead"* (1 Corinthians 15:20). Since all the writers affirm the resurrection of Jesus, this becomes another pillar of evidence to support the fact that Jesus did rise from the dead.

The Reality of Christian Experience

The resurrection of Christ means that Jesus is alive and active today. He is not merely limited to the pages of history. He changes the lives of those who follow Him today. He still helps drunkards sober up, thieves to steal no more, those who hate to develop a heart of love, and those in darkness to be full of light. Jesus is alive! How He is changing people today is evidence that He is risen.

The resurrection of Christ gives believers many assurances in their faith journey. The first assurance is that we worship a living God. Our deity is not some lifeless idol, but alive and involved in our lives. Many other religious leaders lived and died, but Jesus rose again. The second assurance is that we know there is life after death. Jesus proved it with His resurrection. The third assurance is that we know there is a resurrection. Jesus said: *"Destroy this temple and I will raise it again in three days"* (John 2:19). Jesus predicted and proved that there is a resurrection. The fourth assurance is that we know that Jesus is who He claims to be. His resurrection gives credibility to His claims. The fifth assurance we have from the resurrection of Jesus is that we know that there will be a judgment. Scripture is serious when it says that *"just as man is destined to die once, and after that to face judgment"* (Hebrews 9:27). The sixth assurance we have in the resurrection is that our faith is useful. *"And if Christ has not been raised, your faith is futile; you are still in your sins"* (1 Corinthians 15:17).

The Claims of Jesus

The life, death, and resurrection of Jesus made Him very unique. However, it is His unique claims that bear our attention. Jesus claimed to be the *"Son of God"* (Matthew 26:63; John 5:25), a claim to deity. The term "son of..." in the Jewish mind did not imply subordination, but equality and identity of nature. "Son of God" is the highest title of deity that only God could possess.

Jesus claimed to be able to forgive sin. *"But so that you may know that the Son of Man has authority on earth to forgive sins..."* (Matthew 9:6) Only God can forgive sins. Jesus claimed to judge the world: *"And he has given him authority to judge because he is the Son of Man ... I judge only as I hear, and my judgment is just, for I seek not to please myself but him who sent me"* (John 5:27,30). Only God can judge the world. Jesus claimed to give eternal life: *"For God so loved the world that he gave his one and only Son, that whoever believes in him shall not perish but have eternal life"* (John 3:16). Eternal life is something only God can give.

Jesus also claimed to be sinless. He said, *"Can any of you prove me guilty of sin?"* (John 8:46, NIC) Only the Holy God is sinless. Jesus claimed to be the Saviour from sins: *"I told you that you would die in your sins; if you do not believe that I am the one I claim to be, you will indeed die in your sins"* (John 8:24). Jesus also claimed to be able to answer prayers: *"And I will do whatever you ask in my name, so that the Son may bring glory to the Father"* (John 14:13). Only the Sovereign Lord can answer prayers.

Jesus claimed to be the Truth: *"I am the way and the truth and the life. No one comes to the Father except through me"* (John 14:6). He also claimed to have all authority. He said to His disciples before He ascended into heaven: *"All authority in heaven and on earth has been given to me"* (Matthew 28:18). He claimed to be one in essence with God: *"I and the Father are one"* (John 10:30). The Jews knew exactly what Jesus meant when He said these things and wanted to stone Him. When Jesus asked His critics for which miracle He had performed they were planning to stone Him for, the Jews replied: *"We are not stoning you for any of these ... but for blasphemy, because you, a mere man, claim to be God"* (John 10:33).

All the claims that Jesus made on the earth were references to deity. The conclusion is that Jesus was either a liar, a lunatic, a legend, or He was who He claimed to be, the Son of God. It would be almost impossible for Jesus to have lied, because it would be inconsistent with His holy life and teachings. Jesus could have been a lunatic. However, again, the impact of the life and teachings of Jesus does not fit the persona of Him being a madman. The possibility that Jesus never made these claims and that His followers just created the idea that He was God, making Him a legend, ignores many scholarly principles. The conclusion is that He must be as He claimed to be: God in human form. He is truly Lord.

The Presence of Jesus

Jesus not only exists in the writings of our history books, but He also exists in the pages of our newspapers today. He told His disciples that He would be going away from them for a little while, but would one day return: *"Do not let your hearts be troubled. Trust in God; trust also in me. In my Father's house are many rooms; if it were not so, I would have told you. I am going there to prepare a place for you. And if I go and prepare a place for you, I will come back and take you to be with me that you also may be where I am"* (John 14:1-3).

Jesus promised His disciples that they would not be alone on this earth. The Holy Spirit would come and be with them and live in them. Jesus said: *"And I will ask the Father, and he will give you another Counselor to be with you forever—the Spirit of truth. The world cannot accept him, because it neither sees him nor knows him. But you know him, for he lives with you and will be in you"* (John 14:16-17).

Christians today have the Spirit of Christ dwelling in them. The New Testament speaks mystically of the Spirit living in us. Paul writes: *"You, however, are controlled not by the sinful nature but by the Spirit, if the Spirit of God lives in you. And if anyone does not have the Spirit of Christ, he does not belong to Christ. But if Christ is in you, your body is dead because of sin, yet your spirit is alive because of righteousness. And if the Spirit of him who raised Jesus from the dead is living in you, he who raised Christ from the dead will also give life to your mortal bodies through his Spirit, who lives in you"* (Romans 8:9-11).

Another perspective of a believer's relationship to Christ is that Christians are the ones who are "in Christ." Paul addressed the believers in Colossae as *"the holy and faithful brothers in Christ"* (Colossians 1:2). He also addressed the Philippian Christians as *"saints in Christ Jesus"* (Philippians 1:1). The language of Christ living in a believer and a believer being in Christ speaks of the intimate relationship we are to have with Jesus Christ. Jesus is alive today, and wants to be with us and in us. We need to acknowledge His Spirit and His presence until He physically and bodily returns one day!

Questions to Ponder

1. What about Jesus catches your attention?
2. What aspect(s) of Jesus' death do you find bears repeating?
3. Why is the resurrection of Jesus Christ relevant to you today?
4. What amazes you about the claims of Jesus?
5. Is the presence of Jesus a reality in your life?

CHAPTER FIVE

Discover Love

A survey was once given, asking the question, "If there is one thing in life you could have, what would it be?" The overwhelming answer from respondents was "love." To most people, the desire to love and be loved is deeper than any other. Many people live in a world that is void of love. They have experienced loveless relationships. Some grew up in broken homes where self-preservation was the key to survival, while others grew up in homes that seemed outwardly like normal families, but were actually full of discouragement and bitterness. Some have seen their romances turn into disappointment, while still others have tried to exist in a cold, competitive world that treats them as a number and statistic. It is therefore not surprising to find that many people in our world are lonely, desperately wanting to love and be loved.

We all need love. From the time we are born into this world, we need to be held, touched, and loved by our parents. Most parents do love their children, but often they do not know how to express their love in a manner that lets the child feel loved. As a result, many people grow up yearning for the love they lacked as children.

Some people look for love by being involved in various relationships, going from one person to another, while others search for true love and intimacy by engaging in all manner of sexual activity. Some people have tried to make as much money as possible in order for them to be able to buy their own love and happiness, while others turn to accomplishments in the game of life to find acceptance. Yet these attempts for love often leave deeper wounds, a feeling of purposelessness, and a profound sense of loneliness and emptiness. The hurt and loneliness can sometimes be so intense that people indulge in a particular hobby or habit to erase the pain of not knowing true love.

Is love the end of the rainbow we never find? Is it an ideal dream that belongs only to the world of fables and fairytales? The Apostle John makes an interesting statement about love in one of his letters. He writes, *"Whoever does not love does not know God, because God is love"* (1 John 4:8). Later on in the letter, John says, *"And so we know and rely on the love God has for us. God is love. Whoever lives in love lives in God, and God in him"* (1 John 4:16).

God does more than know love and express love; He *is* love. God is love in His nature and His character. At the very essence of God is love. At the very essence of love is God. To understand and experience God is to know love. To understand and experience love is to know God. When people try to love without God, they love in a vacuum. God has created and designed us to love when we are connected to Him. It is only when we have His Spirit in us that we can truly love our neighbours. It is only through His Spirit that He can help us to truly love our enemies.

How can we truly love? If God is love, how can He erase the pain, bitterness, and loneliness that has been built up over the years? How can we connect with God to the point where we can truly love our neighbours and enemies?

Loving God

The first love relationship we all need is with God. Our love relationship with God is the Father of all relationships. When people are connected with God, they are also connected with an endless source of love for other relationships. A love relationship with God begins by understanding, receiving, and responding to His love for us.

The Old Testament contains many words that express the idea of love. *'Ahab* is mostly used to express human love towards God, people, family, friends, and things. It was used in the context of human love between a man and a woman, such as in the case of Jacob being "in love" with Rachel (Genesis 29:18). *'Ahab* was also used to described the human love between family members, as in the case of Israel, who *"loved Joseph more than any of his other sons"* (Genesis 37:3). It can also be used as human love for an object or a belief such as in the command, *"seek good, not evil"* (Amos 5:14). *'Ahab* has also been used to express our human love towards God. *"Love the LORD your God with all your heart and with all your soul and with all your strength"* (Deuteronomy 6:5).

Two words in the Old Testament are often used to express God's love for man. The Hebrew word *racham* means to love, love deeply, have mercy, be compassionate, have tender affection, or have compassion. *"Then the LORD your God will restore your fortunes and have compassion on you..."* (Deuteronomy 30:3). Another Hebrew word that expresses God's love is *checed*, meaning goodness, kindness, and faithfulness. *"For great is His love towards us"* (Psalm 117:2). God's love expressed in the Old Testament is often in the context of mercy, compassion, goodness, loving kindness, and faithfulness.

Ancient Greek literature has three words that convey the idea of love. One Greek word, *eros*—from which we get the word 'erotic'—refers to romantic or sexual love, and is not found in the New Testament. Another Greek word, *phileo*, means to love, approve of, like, sanction, treat affectionately or kindly, welcome, befriend, show signs of love to, or kiss. It is often used in the context of brotherly love, as in Titus' letter: *"Greet those who love us in the faith"* (Titus 3:15). For this reason, Philadelphia is known as 'the city of brotherly love.'

A third Greek word which means 'love,' appears rarely in ancient Greek literature, but quite often in the New Testament. It is *agape*. *Agape* love can also mean brotherly love, affection, goodwill, love, or benevolence. What distinguishes *agape* love from *phileo* love is that *agape* is almost always associated with God's love, which is described as perfect. *"There is no fear in love. But perfect love drives out fear, because fear has to do with punishment. The one who fears is not made perfect in love"* (1 John 4:18). *Agape* love is seen as sacrificial love. *"Greater love has no one than this, that he lay down his life for his friends"* (John 15:13). God's love is also an unconditional love. He loves us in spite of our rebellion against Him: *"But God demonstrates his own love for us in this: While we were still sinners, Christ died for us"* (Romans 5:8).

The Bible clearly shows that God's love is the highest form of love anyone can experience. It involves mercy, compassion, goodness, kindness, and faithfulness, expressed in fearless, unconditional, and sacrificial perfection. It is never selfish, but always selfless. God's love is patient and kind: *"It does not envy, it does not boast, it is not proud. It is not rude, it is not self-seeking, it is not easily angered, it keeps no record of wrongs. Love does not delight in evil but rejoices with the truth. It always protects, always trusts, always hopes, always perseveres"* (1 Corinthians 13:4-7).

Our minds must begin to grasp the magnitude of God's merciful love. However, a relationship with the Creator is more than a mere intellectual exercise. A relationship with God must penetrate deep to the core of one's soul and one's spirit, leaving us emotionally drained in the end—yet spiritually satisfying. Consider the Psalmist, who had a taste of a connection with God and yet thirsted for more: *"As the deer pants for streams of waters, so my soul pants for you, O God. My soul thirsts for God, for the living God. When can I go and meet with God?"* (Psalms 42:1-2)

It is when we begin to grasp, understand, and experience God's merciful love that we can then respond to God in love. God's love encompasses us and overwhelms us so much that we must respond in gratitude and worship: *"Because your love is better than life, my lips will glorify you"* (Psalm 63:3).

The summary of the law in the Old Testament was to choose to love God: *"This day I call heaven and earth as witnesses against you that I have set before you life and death, blessings and curses. Now choose life, so that you and your children may live and that you may love the LORD your God, listen to his voice, and hold fast to him"* (Deuteronomy 30:19-20a). Our love for God means that we hate what is evil: *"Let those who love the LORD hate evil, for he guards the lives of his faithful ones and delivers them from the hand of the wicked"* (Psalm 97:10).

An expert in the law once tested Jesus by asking Him, *"'Which is the greatest commandment in the Law?' Jesus replied, 'Love the Lord your God with all your heart and with all soul and with all your mind. This is the first and greatest commandment'"* (Matthew 22:36-38). Our capacity to truly love unconditionally, sacrificially, and perfectly must begin with God's love melting our hearts. It is when we are in love with God, being saturated with Him, that we have the power to truly love others.

Loving Our Neighbours

Many people do not have a problem with loving God. After all, God is love. However, when it comes to loving others, many do have a problem. For some, loving their neighbours really depends on who their neighbours are.

Another young lawyer wanted to sharpen his intellect with Jesus. He came to Jesus and asked Him,

> "What must I do to inherit eternal life?"
> "What is written in the Law?" he replied. "How do you read it?"
> He answered: "'Love the Lord your God with all your heart and with all your soul and with all your strength and with all your mind'; and, 'Love your neighbor as yourself.'"

"You have answered correctly," Jesus replied. "Do this and you will live."

But he wanted to justify himself, so he asked Jesus, "And who is my neighbour?" (Luke 10:25-29)

The young lawyer wanted to test Jesus. He knew that the central theme of the law was to love God and to love one's neighbour. Jesus agreed with the lawyer's response and told him that if he did this, he would have that eternal life. The lawyer believed that he could produce evidence in his life to prove his love for God. However, he knew that he could not produce evidence to show that he loved his neighbours. It was as if he had just created his own exam, and then miserably flunked it. Here was a clear requirement from God that was not obeyed. He felt convicted and wanted to justify himself and asked, "Who is my neighbour?"

Jesus did not respond with abstract theories on love. Instead, He told a story of a man who was mugged and left for dead. He spoke of a world where people can get robbed, beaten, and even murdered. He replied to the lawyer with the following story:

"A man was going down from Jerusalem to Jericho, when he fell into the hands of robbers. They stripped him of his clothes, beat him and went away, leaving him half dead. A priest happened to be going down the same road, and when he saw the man, he passed by on the other side. So too, a Levite, when he came to the place and saw him, passed by on the other side. But a Samaritan, as he traveled, came where the man was; and when he saw him, he took pity on him. He went to him and bandaged his wounds, pouring on oil and wine. Then he put the man on his own donkey, took him to an inn and took care of him. The next day he took out two silver coins and gave them to the innkeeper. 'Look after him,' he said, 'and when I return, I will reimburse you for any extra expense you may have.'" (Luke 10:30-35)

The Identity of Neighbours

Who is your neighbour? The identity of a neighbour depends on who and where you are. If you are visiting a friend who lives in a small unfamiliar village where you have never been before, everyone will be a stranger. However, everyone in that village would consider your friend a neighbour. Who your neighbour is, then, depends on who and where you are. If you were the wounded traveler, your definition of neighbour would be anyone who is willing to help. I was once fishing with a friend when the motor on our boat died right in the middle of a lake. Our definition of neighbour then was anyone who was able to come by and help.

In the story that Jesus told the young lawyer, there were several candidates who could have been the neighbour. The top candidate, someone who you would think would come by and help, was the priest. After all, he was in the practice of helping people out. A priest would quote Scripture every morning: *"Hear, O Israel: The LORD our God, the LORD is one. Love the LORD your God with all your heart and with all your soul and with all your strength"* (Deuteronomy 6:4-5). He knew and practiced the parts about loving God. He probably justified walking by the wounded traveller because of his responsibilities. The priest was probably thinking that the man looked dead or almost dead. If he were to get involved, the man might even die in his arms. Then he would have touched a dead body, making him ceremonially unclean and therefore unable to perform the rites of the temple. After all, He was obeying the Lord by avoiding the dead body, for priests *"must not enter a place where there is a dead body. He must not make himself unclean, even for his father or mother, nor leave the sanctuary of his God or desecrate it, because he has been dedicated by the anointing oil of his God"* (Leviticus 21:11-12). Helping the wounded traveller would have caused a great deal of inconvenience and raised too many questions about why he made himself unclean.

A second top candidate for helping the neighbour was the Levite. He too was most likely on his way to a meeting at the temple in Jerusalem. Perhaps he thought that the robbers were still around and cautiously passed by on the other side of the road. More likely, the Levite did not have the time to get involved with this wounded traveller. He probably had people to see and things to do. The wounded traveller would have delayed him and altered his plans that day. In a different time and under different circumstance, the Levite might have helped.

The Samaritan, in contrast, was probably at the bottom of the list of possible candidates for helping his neighbour. Samaritans were half-Jews and seen as "dogs." Yet when he saw a stranger in need, he helped him. To the wounded traveler, a neighbour was anyone who would come by and help. To the Samaritan, a neighbour was anyone he came across in need of his help.

Who is your neighbour? Your neighbour is anyone you come across and are able to help. He or she can be a total stranger. Your neighbour could be someone you think is unfriendly, unlovely, unattractive, or unrewarding to be involved with.

The Involvement with Neighbours

What does it take to love your neighbour? First, it requires involvement with your neighbour in the giving of your time. The road to Jerusalem was known to have robbers, and the Samaritan would have had good reason to suspect that they were lurking around. Nonetheless, he went out of his way to spend time with this stranger. Loving anyone requires spending time with them. Loving a neighbour requires our time, even at the cost of our own convenience.

Second, loving your neighbour requires your involvement in the giving of your resources. The Samaritan was willing to give two silver coins, which was two *denarii*—the equivalent of two days' wages. There are times when loving our neighbours means parting with our money or resources. Loving our neighbour, then, means being involved with them, both in terms of our time and resources.

The Instruction about Neighbours

Why then is it so hard for many of us to love our neighbours? It certainly is more than seeing the needs of the homeless, the poor, the troubled, and unlovable around us. It is not enough to simply see the need of those around us. The priest saw the need of the wounded traveler, but he also saw the potential uncleanness of the situation. The Levite saw the need of the wounded traveler, but he also saw the inconvenience of getting involved. If others were to travel on the same road that day, everyone would have seen the same need of the wounded traveler. The difference that determined how the different men acted lay in who they were. The priest and the Levite were very religious indeed, but they did not have the love of God in them. The Samaritan had the love of God in him and was able to act lovingly.

The emphasis here is not on the object of love but on the one who loves. What you are determines how you love and how you act. A person who is not connected with God and does not know His love will have a difficult time loving his neighbour. In contrast, a person who knows God and is saturated with God's love will be able to love his neighbour unconditionally. What you are inside determines what you see and do.

We are created to be creatures of love. First to love God, and second to love our neighbours. It is very difficult to love our neighbours unconditionally without first loving God. Love is the main characteristic of a Christian. You can tell whether or not a person is a Christian by the love he or she demonstrates. A person is not necessarily a Christian just because he claims to be one. A person is not necessarily a Christian just because he attends church, does good works, and obeys the commandments. A person is not necessarily a Christian just because he belongs to a religious group, like the priest or Levite did, or just because he holds onto a set of religious beliefs. Only love marks the Christian. Jesus said, *"A new command I give you: Love one another. As I have loved you, so you must love one another. By this all men will know that you are my disciples, if you love one another"* (John 13:34-35). The real sign of a Christian is God-given *agape* love—love that is unselfish, unconditional, sacrificial, and perfect in its expression, even to strangers.

Loving Our Enemies

How far does God's love take us? Jesus gave us a new perspective on love. He taught:

> "You have heard that it was said, 'Love your neigh-
> bor and hate your enemy.' But I tell you: Love your

enemies and pray for those who persecute you, that
you may be sons of your Father in heaven. He causes
his sun to rise on the evil and the good, and sends
rain on the righteous and the unrighteous. If you love
those who love you, what reward will you get? Are
not even the tax collectors doing that? And if you
greet only your brothers, what are you doing more
than others? Do not even pagans do that? Be perfect,
therefore, as your heavenly Father is perfect." (Matthew 5:43-48)

The traditional religious teaching of the time was to "love your
neighbour and hate your enemy." This is a natural aspect of love, for it
is easy in almost every culture to justify loving one's neighbour and
hating one's enemy. However, what Jesus taught was not natural. The
idea of loving one's enemies and praying for those who persecute you
goes against every grain of our human nature. Loving those who love
you and greeting only your brothers are examples of natural love.
Loving one's enemies takes supernatural love. Only with God's
supernatural love can we even begin to love our enemies.

The idea of loving one's enemies has several implications to us
loving our neighbours. First, it means that the identity of neighbour
extend even to our enemies. Consider God's love for us: *"When we
were God's enemies, we were reconciled to him through the death of
his Son..."* (Romans 5:10) If this is the case, that we are to love those
who hate, despise, and persecute us, then loving our neighbour means
loving everyone we come across and is in need of our help.

Secondly, loving our enemies means that our love for one another
must be unconditional. The emphasis is no longer on the one who is
loved, but on the lover. Real love towards another is never *if* or *because*
that individual meets certain conditions. God's love is never, "I love
him if...," or "I love him because...," but "I love him, period." No
conditions should ever be attached to our love for our neighbours.

Thirdly, loving our enemies implies that our love must be a
supernatural love. Our human ability to love others is limited. True
unconditional, sacrificial, and selfless *agape* love requires the Spirit of

love. When Jesus tells us to be perfect like the Heavenly Father is perfect, we acknowledge that we cannot display this perfect love without some kind of supernatural intervention. Once again, we cannot experience true love without our Creator. *"God is love. Whoever lives in love lives in God, and God in him"* (1 John 4:16).

God loves you and created you to be loved and to love. Have you ever considered true love in relation to the source of love? God wants to saturate you with His love and give you the love that so overflows to the point where you love even your enemies. True love is not godless, but God-centred. At the heart of Christianity is the true experience of God's love.

Questions to Ponder

1. What did you learn about love?
2. How far can a person love without God?
3. What is the difference between God's love and human love?
4. Who is your neighbour?
5. Do you have difficulty loving your neighbour? Why?

CHAPTER SIX
Discover Forgiveness

The head of a mental institution once said, "I could release half my patients if they knew how to get rid of guilt." People not only feel guilty about their sins; they are guilty of their sins. We all respond to guilt in different ways. Some people deny their guilt. They refuse to respect the law and the lawgivers who reveal their guilt. People who deny that they are guilty of certain sins will try to excuse their sin, because the law did not fit into their circumstance. Some people reject God and the Bible because God's Word shows them that they are guilty of sin, and they do not want to be reminded of it. The Bible speaks of those who suppress the truth, wanting to continue to indulge in their sins. *"The wrath of God is being revealed from heaven against all the godlessness and wickedness of men who suppress the truth by their wickedness, since what may be known about God is plain to them, because God has made it plain to them"* (Romans 1:18-19).

A similar response to guilt is to hide the guilt. Some ignore the guilt and hope it goes away, or hide it so that not too many people will notice. King David was guilty of adultery with Bathsheba. When

Bathsheba told David that she was pregnant by him, David tried to cover up their sin by sending Uriah, Bathsheba's husband, back home in the hope that Uriah would sleep with his wife. When the attempted cover-up failed, David ordered Uriah to the front lines of the battle, where he was eventually killed (2 Samuel 11). Guilt never goes away when we try to ignore it or hide it from others.

Another response to guilt is to shift the blame to someone else. When Adam was confronted by the Lord concerning his disobedience in eating from the tree he was commanded not to eat from, he refused to take responsibility for his own sin. Adam said: *"The woman you put here with me—she gave me some fruit from the tree, and I ate it"* (Genesis 3:12). Adam tried to shift the focus on the woman, and even to God Himself. He said that it was *"you"* (God) who put her here with me. People who blame others for their own guilt have a difficult time taking responsibility for their own sins.

The story has been told of a young twelve-year-old boy who was throwing stones outside his home, accidentally killing one of the family geese by hitting it squarely in the head. The young boy buried the dead bird, hoping that his parents would not notice that one of the twenty-four birds was missing. However, that evening, his sister called him aside and said, "I saw what you did. If you don't offer to do the dishes tonight, I'll tell Mother." The next morning, the boy's sister blackmailed him into washing the dishes again. His guilt was a chain that bound him to do the dishes.

Many people today are confined because of their guilt. Some have spent much time and money trying to get rid of it from their lives, and yet it keeps coming back. Others feel so guilty of what they have done that they are determined to live a torturous life in order to punish themselves for their sins. What is God's answer to guilt?

The Forgiving Father

Christianity is all about getting rid of guilt and sin. The solution to guilt is to be forgiven. Jesus had much to say about forgiveness. He taught and told many stories related to forgiveness. The most beautiful story was about a lost son in Luke. Jesus said:

There was a man who had two sons. The younger one said to his father, "Father, give me my share of the estate." So he divided his property between them.

Not long after that, the younger son got together all he had, set off for a distant country and there squandered his wealth in wild living. After he had spent everything, there was a severe famine in that whole country and he began to be in need. So he went and hired himself out to a citizen of that country, who sent him to his fields to feed pigs. He longed to fill his stomach with the pods that the pigs were eating, but no one gave him anything.

When he came to his senses, he said, "How many of my father's hired men have food to spare, and here I am starving to death! I will set out and go back to my father and say to him: Father, I have sinned against heaven and against you. I am no longer worthy to be called your son; make me like one of your hired men." So he got up and went to his father.

But while he was still a long way off, his father saw him and was filled with compassion for him; he ran to his son, threw his arms around him and kissed him.

The son said to him, "Father, I have sinned against heaven and against you. I am no longer worthy to be called your son."

But the father said to his servants, "Quick! Bring the best robe and put it on him. Put a ring on his finger and sandals on his feet. Bring the fattened calf and kill it. Let's have a feast and celebrate. For this son of mine was dead and is alive again; he was lost and is found." So they began to celebrate.

Meanwhile, the older son was in the field. When he came near the house, he heard music and dancing. So he called one of the servants and asked him what was going on. "Your brother has come," he replied, "and your father has killed the fattened calf because he has him back safe and sound."

The older brother became angry and refused to go in. So his father went out and pleaded with him. But he answered his father, "Look! All these years I've been slaving for you and never disobeyed your orders. Yet you never gave me even a young goat so I could celebrate with my friends. But when this son of yours who has squandered your property with prostitutes comes home, you kill the fattened calf for him!"

"My son," the father said, "you are always with me, and everything I have is yours. But we had to celebrate and be glad, because this brother of yours was dead and is alive again; he was lost and is found." (Luke 15:11-32).

The Rebellious Son (Verses 11-20)

Jesus introduced to a rebellious son who wanted to manipulate his father. He wanted his share of the inheritance now, instead of waiting to receive it when his father died. In asking for his inheritance, the young son was really telling his father to drop dead. This son did not care much for his father's feelings. He cared only for himself and wanted to be on his own.

The young man's inheritance was land. According to Jewish custom and law, his older brother would get two-thirds of the land and he would get one-third of the land. It was a bold move for the son to go against the patriarchal social custom by asking for the land. And the father, instead of disciplining him, actually gave him the land. Even God the Father recognizes that in parenthood, there is a time to let go!

The young man got together everything he had. The most likely means was that he sold his land for money. He wanted to move away from his father and set off to a distant country (a Jewish term for Gentile-populated areas). The young man wanted to be away from his father's influence. He squandered his wealth in wild living. Rather than invest his inheritance, he spent it all on wild parties and destructive lifestyles. He spent everything he had, leaving himself unprepared for famine.

The young rebel struggled to feed himself. He ran out of money and had to work at the only job he could find, feeding pigs (keep in mind he grew up seeing pigs as filthy, disgusting animals). He noticed that the pigs he was feeding ate better than he did. He longed to eat what the pigs ate, yet no one gave him anything to eat.

He decided to make up with his father. The story says that he "came to his senses." The young son remembered his father and His father's servants. He acknowledged his sorry condition and decided to go back to his father. He was planning to confess his sins to his father. He had a speech all pre-planned, saying: "Father I have sinned against heaven and against you." This was more than just saying "I'm sorry." The young son concluded that he could only come back as a servant. He planned to acknowledge that he was no longer worthy to be called his father's son. The young man concluded that he could only come back as a hired house servant or skilled labourer, and not as a son. He determined to earn back what he had lost, and possibly even earn back his father's favour. Instead of just thinking about it, the young son got up and went to his father.

The Repentant Son (Verses 20-24)

The repentant son experienced the Father's compassion. His father was waiting in his fenced-in community when he saw his son. He must have recognized his son's walk. When the father saw him, he was already waiting for him. The father was full of compassion for his son. He ran and threw his arms around him and kissed him. It was socially immoral for a man to expose his legs in public in Jesus' day, yet the father must have lifted up his robes and exposed his legs when he ran to his son. The father did not care about what other people thought when he showed his love for his son. Perhaps he wanted to get to his son before the townspeople approached him and humiliated him for losing his money to Gentiles. The townspeople could have forced the son to be an outcast in the village, but the father loved the rebellious son so much that he would even go through humiliation for his return. This is a picture of how much God the Father loves us and is waiting for us in rebellion to come home

The repentant son experienced the Father's forgiveness. The father acknowledged his runaway child as a son. The father called the young repentant rebel "this son of mine," along with all the hugs and kisses. He did not despise or disown his son for what he had done, but related to him as a son. When we experience the forgiveness of God, we are treated as sons and daughters of God, and not as hired help.

The repentant son experienced the Father's grace. Grace is receiving what we do not deserve. The best robe was put on the son. Usually the robe was given to the guest of honour. The sandals on his feet would have been sandals only a free man could wear. The ring on his finger was the signet ring of authority. The father gave all the privileges and rights to the son. The fattened calf was killed only on very special occasions. People in the first century did not eat meat regularly. But on this occasion, they all enjoyed a feast. It was an unexpected party and there were many reasons to rejoice. They began to celebrate because a son who had been dead was now alive. He had been lost, but now was found. When a sinner comes home to the Father, He does not humiliate him by putting him in the position of a hired hand, but rejoices and gives him the full status and privileges of a son.

The Raging Son (Verses 25-32)

It is interesting that Jesus did not end the story of the lost son with the celebration. The rebellious son had an older brother who would have been considered "the good son" by every standard. Even though outwardly the older son seemed to have a better relationship with his father, the facts show otherwise. The older son was the self-righteous, raging son.

The raging son was angry with his Father. He was jealous of his younger brother. The older son refused to go into the party. He had never had a party thrown for him. He had never had a goat prepared for him, never mind the fattened calf. He was judgmental toward his brother. He referred to his brother as "this son of yours," and not "my brother." He said that his brother had squandered his father's property with prostitutes. This may have only been what he heard or made up absent of concrete facts. The older brother was angry with his Father for welcoming his younger brother home.

The raging son was arguing with his father. He talked about the righteous life he had led. He said: "I've been slaving for you all these years ... I've never disobeyed your orders." He talked about the rewards he lacked. He pointed out to his father that he had never been given a goat so that he could celebrate with his friends. What the older son was saying was that he really deserved the fattened calf. He talked about the resources he would lose. The older son pointed out to the father that his younger son had squandered his property, but now he wanted to move in on his older brother's inheritance. What the older son was saying was that the father's young son was freeloading. The father killed the fattened calf for the younger son, while the older son had probably had plans for that calf.

The raging son was alienated from his father. He failed to see his father's presence. The father reassured him of his presence saying, "My son, you are always with me." The older son also failed to see his father's possessions. The father reaffirmed to the older son that he was still the heir by saying: "Everything I have is yours." He failed to see his father's passion. The father pointed out, "This brother of yours, not just my son, was dead to us and is alive again. He was lost to us and is found again."

The two sons related to the father differently. The rebellious son became the repentant son. He had hurt his father greatly but changed his mind concerning his rebellion. The repentant son truly experienced the father's love, forgiveness, and grace. This put him in a right relationship with God. The raging son, on the other hand, did not experience the forgiveness of God. He was self-righteous and outwardly seemed to have a healthy relationship with the father. However, the older son was not close to the father at all. He did not have the father's heart for those who were dead and lost.

This story that Jesus shared was told in the context of the despised tax collectors and sinners who gathered around Jesus to hear His teachings. The religious leaders of the day severely criticized Jesus saying: *"This man welcomes sinners and eats with them"* (Luke 15:2). The religious leaders missed the point: it was the "sinners" who needed the forgiveness of God. Sinners who experience the forgiveness of God are much closer to the Father than those who are outwardly religious, but inwardly do not know the Father's heart.

The Forgiving Child

The Father's forgiveness is only one aspect of forgiveness. The other aspect of forgiveness deals with our forgiveness in response to the Father's forgiveness. We have not truly understood the implications of God's forgiveness if we do not forgive. Consider what Jesus said: *"For if you forgive men when they sin against you, your heavenly Father will also forgive you. But if you do not forgive men their sins, your Father will not forgive your sins"* (Matthew 6:14-15) Jesus taught us to pray, *"Forgive us our debts, as we also have forgiven our debtors"* (Matthew 6:12) Once again, Jesus taught us that our sins have put us into a great moral and legal debt. The Father has forgiven us and atoned for our sins through the death of His Son. Since he has paid our debts, it is only fitting that we cancel the moral debts we feel are owed to us. The following passage from Matthew has much to say about forgiveness:

> Then Peter came to Jesus and asked, "Lord, how many times shall I forgive my brother when he sins against me? Up to seven times?"
>
> Jesus answered, "I tell you, not seven times, but seventy-seven times.
>
> "Therefore, the kingdom of heaven is like a king who wanted to settle accounts with his servants. As he began the settlement, a man who owed him ten thousand talents was brought to him. Since he was

not able to pay, the master ordered that he and his wife and his children and all that he had be sold to repay the debt.

"The servant fell on his knees before him. 'Be patient with me,' he begged, 'and I will pay back everything.' The servant's master took pity on him, canceled the debt and let him go.

"But when that servant went out, he found one of his fellow servants who owed him a hundred denarii. He grabbed him and began to choke him. 'Pay back what you owe me!' he demanded.

"His fellow servant fell to his knees and begged him, 'Be patient with me, and I will pay you back.'" But he refused. Instead, he went off and had the man thrown into prison until he could pay the debt. When the other servants saw what had happened, they were greatly distressed and went and told their master everything that had happened.

"Then the master called the servant in. 'You wicked servant,' he said, 'I canceled all that debt of yours because you begged me to. Shouldn't you have had mercy on your fellow servant just as I had on you?' In anger his master turned him over to the jailers to be tortured, until he should pay back all he owed.

"This is how my heavenly Father will treat each of you unless you forgive your brother from your heart." (Matthew 18:21-35)

The Problem with Forgiveness (Verses 21-22)

Peter asked Jesus, "Lord, how many times shall I forgive my brother when he sins against me?" Many can identify with Peter because it is hard to forgive someone again and again. Peter thought that he was being very generous in saying up to seven times. However, Jesus pointed out that we should forgive seventy-seven times. He was not suggesting that after four hundred and ninety times, we can stop forgiving, but that forgiveness should be limitless.

There are many people who in their minds accept the forgiveness of God, but have difficulty forgiving themselves or others. There are some people who say they accept the forgiveness of God, but they do not forgive themselves. They believe that their sin is so severe that they need to be punished. The problem is that they have not truly experienced the forgiveness of God that removes their guilt. By punishing themselves for their own sins, they are really saying that Christ's punishment on the cross was not enough for them.

There are others who say they accept the forgiveness of God, but they cannot forgive those who offend them. This is a real misunderstanding of how much grace we have received from God. It is easier for prodigal children, who have received much grace from God, to forgive others than for self-righteous religionists, who do not forgive their brothers.

The Parable of Forgiveness (Verses 23-34)

Jesus talked about the kingdom being like a king who wanted to settle accounts with his servants. A certain man owed the king 10,000 talents and was unable to pay it. The king ordered that the man and his wife, along with their children be sold to repay the debt. The man pleaded and begged for mercy and the king cancelled the man's debt. When the servant went out, he found a fellow servant that owed him an amount significantly less than that which he had owed the king. The man who had been forgiven by the king of the great debt could not find it in himself to forgive the smaller debts owed to him. Instead, he had the man thrown in jail until he could pay the small debt. This not only disturbed the other servants, but it bothered the king, who eventually heard about it. The king called the servant "wicked" and threw him into jail until he could pay back all that he owed.

The Point of Forgiveness (Verse 35)

The king in the parable is God, who has forgiven us of the great debt of our sin. How can we not forgive our offenders, whose sin against us is comparatively so small? How can we expect God to forgive us when we cannot forgive others? How can a person claim to have the forgiveness of God and remain bitter against a parent, leader, boss, peer, brother, or sister? Those who truly have God's forgiveness should not hesitate to forgive themselves and others.

The Practice of Forgiveness

First, realize your need for the Father's forgiveness. Humble yourself as the repentant son and realize that you are at His mercy because of your sins. Everyone who receives the forgiveness of God must realize that they are deep in the debt of sin and at the mercy of God.

Second, accept the Father's forgiveness. Accept in your heart that God has paid for your debt of sin through the death of His Son, Jesus. Accept the fact that Jesus died for your sins and took your place on the cross.

Third, forgive yourself for your sins. Understand that Jesus was the substitute for your sins. That means His death was enough to satisfy the wrath of God. If God has forgiven you, who are you not to forgive yourself?

Fourth, forgive others who have offended you. Realize that God is using your offender to develop your character. Thank God for those lessons in offense. Yield all your rights to God, especially your right to your opinions without being "jumped on," or your right to be accepted as an individual.

Often we feel we have rights to our own personal free time, to privacy, to earn and spend money, to choose our friends, to our personal belongings, and to be in control. It is hard to forgive others. That's why when we become children of God, God gives us His Spirit. His Spirit dwells within us and helps us to forgive. One of the fruits of the Spirit is love (Galatians 5:22). The act of forgiveness is an act of love. Jesus said: *"Blessed are the merciful, for they will be shown mercy"* (Matthew 5:7). Realize that *"judgment without mercy will be shown to anyone who has not been merciful. Mercy triumphs over judgment!"* (James 2:13)

The Solution to Guilt

God's solution to remove guilt is His forgiveness. A person who has truly experienced the forgiveness of God is able to also forgive others. True freedom from all guilt is found in the forgiveness the Father gives through Jesus Christ.

The story of the boy who accidentally killed and buried the goose found freedom. As long as he wanted to keep his guilt hidden, his sister would keep blackmailing him into washing the dishes. On the third day of the blackmail, the young boy surprised his sister by telling her it was her turn to wash the dishes. When she tried to remind him of what she could do in revealing his secret, he replied, "I've already told Mother, and she has forgiven me. Now you do the dishes. I'm free again!"

Our guilt in respect to the law of sin condemns us to death. However, *"there is now no condemnation for those who are in Christ Jesus, because through Christ Jesus the law of the Spirit of life set me free from the law of sin and death"* (Romans 8:1-2). When we have God's forgiveness, no one can condemn us with our guilt. We are free from guilt! We are free from sin! We are free from death!

Questions to Ponder

1. How have you been dealing with your guilt?
2. What aspect(s) of forgiveness touched you?
3. Who can you better identify with, the older son or the younger son?
4. Are you finding it hard to practice forgiveness? Why?
5. What must you do today with your guilt?

CHAPTER SEVEN

Discover the Good News!

Jesus started His ministry preaching the gospel, the good news! What is the Good News of the Bible? This is the same gospel that the Apostles preached everywhere they went. It is the same good news that has changed millions of lives around the world. It is this good news that is light in darkness, hope to those in despair, life to the lifeless. The Apostle Paul pointed out to the Corinthians: *"Now, brothers, I want to remind you of the gospel I preached to you, which you received and on which you have taken your stand. By this gospel you are saved, if you hold firmly to the word I preached to you. Otherwise, you have believed in vain"* (1 Corinthians 15:1-2).

A rich young ruler once asked Jesus an interesting question: *"What good thing must I do to get eternal life?"* (Matthew 19:16) The young man had many things going in his favour. He had great wealth. Not only was he wealthy, he was very wealthy (Matthew 19:22). He was described as a young man (Matthew 19:20), which meant that he had youth and health. The young man also had position. He was described as a ruler (Luke 18:18), probably a ruler in a local synagogue—a very honoured position for a young man. The young man also had influence. He was a respected religious leader who was devout, honest, wealthy, prominent, and influential. He was the kind of young man many parents would want their daughters to bring home. This young man also had initiative. He was the one who came to Jesus and started the conversation.

However, the rich young ruler sincerely felt that something was missing in his life. He asked: "What good thing must I *do* to get eternal life?" He still felt he did not have eternal life. There was emptiness in spite of all his possessions, emptiness in spite of all his position, and emptiness in spite of all his power. In the eyes of the world, he had everything to live for, but in his own eyes his life was empty.

Many people today have asked this common question: *How can I have eternal life?* It is common for people of different backgrounds, ages, and walks of life to desire eternal life. Men and women have been seeking salvation, heaven, and the kingdom of God since the dawn of creation. Central to the teachings of Jesus is the truth about eternal life in the kingdom of heaven. How can we have life everlasting? The Bible tells us what we must do to get eternal life. Consider the following:

Realize Your Condition

Many people desire eternal life and have tried to do many things to obtain it. However, the Bible clearly shows that we can never obtain eternal life on our own: *"For it is by grace you have been saved, through faith—and this not from yourselves, it is the gift of God—not by works, so that no one can boast"* (Ephesians 2:8-9).

God is a holy God and we have all failed to live up to His standard of perfection. Scripture tells us that we *"all have sinned and fall short of the glory of God"* (Romans 3:23). The Bible tells us that *"the wages of sin is death"* (Romans 6:23). Sin separates us from God and deprives us of eternal life in heaven. God first created man to be under His care.

Our sinfulness moved us from being in a place that was under God into a position over God.

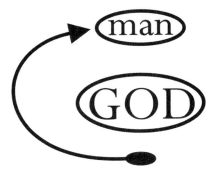

Do you now realize why no one is in a position to earn his or her way to heaven? It is our sin that causes us to miss the mark of holiness. Sin is an addiction that affects our relationship with God. How then can we deal with our sins and get into a right relationship with God?

Repent Of Your Sins

The only way to deal with our sins is to repent of our sins. To repent means to *change our minds* and our hearts from living for ourselves to living for God. It means that we have to come to a realization that we cannot save ourselves and that we are spiritually bankrupt before the Almighty God. In other words, one must admit to God that one's spiritual life is in total disorder and in need of His help.

The rich young ruler did not think he needed to repent of his sins. The young man did not see his own need for a Saviour. He thought that he could earn his salvation and asked: "What *good thing* must I *do* to get eternal life?" The young man was longing to know what good works could bring him the life he was asking for. He saw Jesus as a gifted teacher, but not the one who was good. He was the self-assured guy who thought he could handle whatever instructions Jesus would give him. The young man failed to see his own sinfulness.

Jesus told the young man: *"If you want to enter life, obey the commandments"* (Matthew 19:17). In other words, Jesus was telling the young man that he knew what to do, because it was in the Scriptures. He was a learned and devout Jew who knew what God's law required, so Jesus told him to obey it. The young man responded by asking, "Which ones?" He had read the commandments many times and, as a Jew, had even memorized them as a boy. He had carefully kept them since. He was asking Jesus which of the commandments He had in mind.

Then Jesus quoted five of the Ten Commandments, and "love your neighbor as yourself." No Scripture was more familiar to the young man in his religious upbringing than the ones quoted to him by Jesus. Jesus was trying to show that he could not keep all the commandments perfectly; he could not even keep the ones quoted to him.

The rich young ruler responded: *"All these I have kept ... what do I still lack?"* (Matthew 19:20) The young man had missed the point. He failed to see that the commandments he had learned himself, he had failed to obey. Jesus was trying to point out that if one wants eternal life, one must obey the commandments perfectly. But since the young man lacked this perfect life, he could not have obeyed these commandments perfectly.

There are many religious people who are like the rich young ruler. They fail to see their own sinfulness and their need for a Saviour. They feel that they have it all together spiritually. They would be the ones saying, "What do I still lack?"

Jesus tells us who enters the kingdom of heaven. He said: *"Blessed are the poor in spirit, for theirs is the kingdom of heaven"* (Matthew 5:3). The kingdom belongs to those who are spiritually bankrupt and totally humbled before God. It is not for those who are rich in spirit, thinking that they have it all together spiritually.

When we repent, we change the direction of our lives from a life of sin to a life for God. *"Repent, then, and turn to God, so that your sins may be wiped out, that times of refreshing may come from the Lord"* (Acts 3:19).

"Repent, for the kingdom of heaven is near" (Matthew 4:17) Repentance is not just about feeling sorry for sin. It is more than a few words of confession to ease our conscience. Each one of us needs to repent of trying to be God, and to put oneself willingly under God through Jesus Christ.

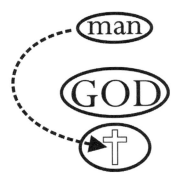

Ask yourself if you have ever repented of your sins. **Have you ever come before God, humbled, in need of His mercy, and desiring His forgiveness?**

Believe In Jesus Christ

When we repent of our sins, we realize that we cannot save ourselves. We must realize that we are in need of a Saviour. That is why Jesus Christ came and died on the cross for our sins and took the punishment for sins that we deserved. We must believe, from our hearts (not just our minds), that Jesus died for our sins and that He rose again three days later to show His power over death. At the heart of the gospel is the death, burial, and resurrection of Jesus Christ. The good news is all about Jesus Christ and how He provides for us to enter the kingdom.

"But God demonstrates his own love for us in this: While we were still sinners, Christ died for us" (Romans 5:8). The Apostle Paul summed up the gospel when he wrote: *"For what I received I passed on to you as of first importance: that Christ died for our sins according*

to the Scriptures, that he was buried, that he was raised on the third day according to the Scriptures" (1 Corinthians 15:3-4).

When a person believes in Jesus Christ, it means that a person puts his or her total trust in Jesus to save him or her from the penalty of his or her sins. It means that the person realizes that his or her eternity is in the hands of Jesus Christ. The person who truly trusts in Jesus to be their Saviour from eternal condemnation will be saved.

"If you confess with your mouth, 'Jesus is Lord,' and believe in your heart that God raised him from the dead, you will be saved. For it is with your heart that you believe and are justified, and it is with your mouth that you confess and are saved" (Romans 10:9-10).

The question is, **have you ever trusted in Christ from your heart for your eternity?** And what does trusting in Christ for your eternity mean?

Follow Jesus Christ

When we want to trust in Christ for our salvation, it also means that we are willing to follow Him for all eternity. Not only do we want to accept Him to be our Savior, but we also acknowledge Him to be our Lord. Accepting Christ means that we also accept who He is and that He is the King of kings and Lord of lords. He is the master, and we are disciples, willing to follow His will for the rest of our lives.

"'Come, follow me,' Jesus said, 'and I will make you fishers of men'" (Matthew 4:19). Jesus said, *"If anyone would come after me, he must deny himself and take up his cross [die to your own self and to your selfish desires] daily and follow me"* (Luke 9:23).

Jesus told the rich young ruler: *"If you want to be perfect, go, sell your possessions and give to the poor, and you will have treasure in heaven. Then come, follow me"* (Matthew 19:21). In other words, if you want to be complete, with eternal life, then go, sell your possessions and give it to the poor. Then, come follow me.

This is the only person in Scripture that Jesus told to sell his possessions. Jesus was testing the man to make him face his own spiritual condition. The young man was self-satisfied with the law. He wanted eternal life on his own terms. He did not think he had any sins to confess. He did not think he was spiritually poor. He thought he was willing to do whatever the Lord required. Jesus told him to prove his sincerity in being willing to do whatever was necessary by selling his possessions and giving it all to the poor.

The real issue with the rich young ruler according to Jesus was: Who is in control of your life—you or me? The complete life is the life where Jesus is in control, where Jesus is master, where Jesus is Lord. That's why He tells many to follow Him.

To follow Jesus is to obey Jesus. To obey Jesus is to obey His word and His will. Obeying Jesus means that you are willing to put Jesus first in your life and to let Him be in control. It is also an expression of love and gratitude for all that Jesus has done for you on the cross. Jesus said: *"If you love me, you will obey what I command"* (John 14:15).

There is a definite difference between those who just profess faith in Christ, but never follow Him, and those who acknowledge Him as Saviour and Lord, and are following Him in obedience.

"Not everyone who says to me, 'Lord, Lord,' will enter the kingdom of heaven, but only he who does the will of my Father who is in heaven" (Matthew 7:21).

Jesus said, *"I have come that they may have life, and have it to the full"* (John 10:10). Do you have this abundant and full life today?

Summary

The gospel must appeal to your mind, emotions, and will. First, you must intellectually find the gospel acceptable. Second, you must be emotionally in want of God's love and forgiveness. Third, you must be willing to become a follower of Jesus. In summary, in order for you to have an abundant and eternal life, you must:

1. Realize you are in no condition to save yourself because of your sins.
2. Repent of your sins and humble yourself before the Almighty God.
3. Believe in your heart that Jesus died for sinners (including you) and rose again to show His power over death.
4. Be willing to follow and obey Him for the rest of your life.

What will keep you from totally following Jesus today? Are you willing to become a Christian now and be a disciple of Jesus Christ? Are you willing to:

1. Repent of your sins?
2. Believe in Jesus Christ?
3. Follow Jesus Christ?

If your answer is **YES** to all three questions, then you can receive Christ right now by praying to God. It is not the words you pray as much as your heart desires that God will hear. The following is a sample prayer that a person can pray to ask Christ to come into one's life.

Dear God,

Thank you for your love! I realize that I have sinned against You. Please forgive me of my sins and have mercy on my soul. I want to repent of my sins and to start anew. I believe that You gave Your Son to die on the cross for my sins. I now realize that His resurrection power is the same power that gives eternal life. I want to follow You from this day forward. Come into my life and be my Master. Help me to be the person you want me to be!

In Jesus' name, Amen.

God's Assurance

If you have prayed this prayer from your heart, consider the following Scriptures:

"Everyone who calls on the name of the Lord will be saved" (Romans 10:13). Only those who have truly called on the name of the Lord will be saved.

"The Spirit himself testifies with our spirit that we are God's children" (Romans 8:16). God gives us His Spirit that dwells in us when we become His children. Is the Spirit of God in you?

"He who has the Son has life; he who does not have the Son of God does not have life. I write these things to you who believe in the name of the Son of God so that you may know that you have eternal life" (1 John 5:12-13). Study the Word of God so that you may know that you have eternal life.

A New Start

If you have made a commitment to Jesus Christ today, congratulations! You are today entering a new phase in your spiritual journey. Mark it down in this book today. Sign on this page as a reminder of your spiritual commitment to Jesus Christ. Have a witness with you to share in your joy! To be a Christian is to be willing to follow Jesus for the rest of your life with the help of the Holy Spirit.

My Commitment

From this day forth, I realize that
I cannot save myself. I know that I have
sinned against the Almighty God and
I repent of my sins.

I have made a commitment today to
receive Jesus Christ as my personal
Saviour and to follow Him as my Lord.

_____   _____
Your Signature   Date

_____
Witness

Now that you have received Christ, this is the beginning of a beautiful relationship with Jesus Christ. In order for you to grow in your relationship with Him, you must:

1. Begin to **read your Bible daily** so that you can know Him better. *"Like newborn babies, crave pure spiritual milk, so that by it you may grow up in your salvation"* (1 Peter 2:2).

2. **Talk to Him in prayer** often about all matters of life. *"Do not be anxious about anything, but in everything, by prayer and petition, with thanksgiving, present your requests to God. And the peace of God, which transcends all understanding, will guard your hearts and your minds in Christ Jesus"* (Philippians 4:6-7).

3. **Share with someone** about your new relationship with Christ. *"But you will receive power when the Holy Spirit comes on you; and you will be my witnesses in Jerusalem, and in all Judea and Samaria, and to the ends of the earth"* (Acts 1:8).

4. Seek to **worship the Lord** with your life. *"Therefore, I urge you, brothers, in view of God's mercy, to offer your bodies as living sacrifices, holy and pleasing to God—this is your spiritual act of worship. Do not conform any longer to the pattern of this world, but be transformed by the renewing of your mind. Then you will be able to test and approve what God's will is—his good, pleasing and perfect will"* (Romans 12:1-2).

5. **Fellowship and grow** with other believers in a Bible-believing church. *"Let us not give up meeting together, as some are in the habit of doing, but let us encourage one another—and all the more as you see the Day approaching"* (Hebrews 10:25).

6. **Love and serve** God with all your heart. *"Love the LORD your God with all your heart and with all your soul and with all your strength"* (Deuteronomy 6:5).

Conclusion

Our recent journey together has taken us to discover God, His Word, the Bible, Jesus, His Love, His forgiveness, and the Good News. Our search for God results in a desire for His glory. The glory of the Lord implies the presence of God among His people. The glory of the Lord was in the tabernacle and the in the temple in the Old Testament. The glory of the Lord was there when Jesus was born. Throughout history, there have been those who desire the glory of God. The reason many do not see the glory of God is because *"all have sinned and fall short of the glory of God"* (Romans 3:23).

Where is the glory of God today? Is the glory in a temple or a church? Remember that the glory of God indicates the presence of God among His people. Jesus said, *"...I am with you always, to the very end of the age"* (Matthew 28:20). God has told His people, *"Never will I leave you; never will I forsake you"* (Hebrews 13:5). If God is with us, then His glory is among us.

Remember that when we become children of God, Christ comes into us and lives in us. Jesus' presence in us is where His glory dwells. The Apostle Paul wrote about a mystery that has been hidden in the dark, but now light is shed upon it. He writes:

> Now I rejoice in what was suffered for you, and I fill up in my flesh what is still lacking in regard to Christ's afflictions, for the sake of his body, which is the church. I have become its servant by the commission God gave me to present to you the word of God in its fullness—the mystery that has been kept hidden for ages and generations, but is now disclosed to the saints. To them God has chosen to make known among the Gentiles the glorious riches of this mystery, which is Christ in you, the hope of glory. (Colossians 1:24-27)

May the Lord bless you with the hope of glory in your spiritual journey!

Questions to Ponder

1. What did you learn about the Good News today?
2. Where are you in your spiritual journey?
3. Are there issues that need to be addressed in your life before you can make a total commitment to Jesus?
4. How can you know that you have eternal life?
5. Is there evidence in your life that Christ is in you?

ABOUT THE AUTHOR

Dr. Kai Mark is an ordained pastor and founder of Unionville Oasis, a unique church in the city of Markham, Ontario. He started his ministry working with high school students for over four years with Ambassadors For Christ and has been a pastor in three different growing churches for over twenty years.

Kai is married to Margaret and they have a son named Gregory and a daughter named Lindsay. Kai has taught as an adjunct faculty at Tyndale University College and Seminary and has over three decades of experience in helping people find God in their spiritual journey.